SHOULDERS

FREDERICK ELOY BOWMAN SR'S LIFE STORY

**A Journey Through Life at an Interesting Time in History
From 1934 Through 2009
From Saginaw, Michigan to Phoenix, Arizona**

SHOULDERS

FREDERICK ELOY BOWMAN SR'S LIFE STORY

A Journey Through Life at an Interesting Time in History
From 1934 Through 2009
From Saginaw, Michigan to Phoenix, Arizona

BY

FREDERICK ELOY BOWMAN, SR.

Bowman Publishing
Phoenix, Arizona

SHOULDERS

FREDERICK ELOY BOWMAN SR.'S LIFE STORY

A Journey Through Life at an Interesting Time in History
From 1934 Through 2009
From Saginaw, Michigan to Phoenix, Arizona

Published by:
Bowman Publishing
fredwildabowman@aim.com

Frederick Eloy Bowman, Sr., Publisher
Quality Press, Production Coordinator

DISCLAIMER:

I have recreated events, locales and conversations from my memories of them. In order to maintain their anonymity in some instances I have changed the names of some individuals and places.

DEDICATION

This book is dedicated to my wife Wilda Bowman (Steptoe), my parents (William and Flora Bowman), Wilda's parents, my grandparents and great grandparents (some of whom I never met), my family and friends, and to all of the many persons on whose shoulders I stand. I also dedicate this book to my children and those who I have been honored to have stand on my shoulders.

SPECIAL ACKNOWLEDGMENT

Before this book was ready for publication, Wilda Delores Bowman, my wife of 50 years, made her transition. While our relationship together is featured throughout the latter half of this book, our day-by-day, moment-by-moment lives together is too great for this modest space. In many ways, my life before her was a divine preparation for our first interaction in 1969 and my life after her was the daily attempt to be the best, most loving version of myself. She deserved no less and gave at least as much in return.

As the author Khalil Gibran suggests, we were "born together, and together {we} shall be forevermore… even in the silent memory of God."

Together, Wilda and I were an unstoppable force, with our love story being that of legend. We were privileged to travel the U.S. and the world together (multiple times over), to bear witness to the successes of our Bowman/Steptoe lineage, and to share our quietest, most vulnerable moments in love. Even though she has left the earthly plane, we are still together.

Wilda Bowman was born in 1942 in Chicago, Illinois to George and Virginia Steptoe. She is survived by me, as well as numerous children, and grandchildren. She is honored by her work with adolescents at several high schools in the greater Phoenix area. She is loved by her church community, as well as her community of friends and extended family. She is missed by all.

This is a small note of love, thanks, and acknowledgment for a woman that was the breath of my life for more than 50 years. There will be a forthcoming book that will chronicle our love in more detail. In the meantime, please know that her story is filled with those that love and appreciate her. My greatest blessing was Wilda.

FOREWORD

When most people think of rising to another level, they think of stairs, ladders, elevators, jumping… or some other type of lifting device comes to mind. Sometimes our thoughts are of hands pulling us up, yet seldom do we think of rising upon people's shoulders. A person's hands can only hold us for a limited time, while shoulders, higher up on the body, are stronger and can withstand weight longer.

Throughout my life, I know that I have stood upon many shoulders when and where my life was challenged and enriched. I have only had the privilege to meet some of those upon whose shoulders I stand. I recognize that they stood tall and allowed me to stand on their shoulders, as they have stood on the shoulders of others. The list goes back in history to my first ancestors, Adam and Eve, the great Kings and Queens of Africa, and Anthony Johnson, the first person of African ancestry, who in 1519 debarked from a Dutch ship onto American soil in Jamestown, and those that followed.

The total number of names would fill volumes of books and many libraries. I am grateful for the opportunities that they afforded me, even when they did not mean me well or their lack of support inspired me to do better and to achieve more. I will always be grateful! This is an effort to honor them through the stories about my life, my challenges and my learning experiences. I hope that someone will be inspired to remember that, regardless of how bleak things may appear, God is always in charge and all is well. We are co-creators of our lives and we can make changes and adjustments while learning to live the life that we desire.

CONTENTS

PART ONE
THIS IS MY LIFE

CHAPTER 1

SAGINAW, MICHIGAN

Saginaw, Michigan is located in the area below the space between the fingers and the thumb on a map of Michigan. It sits along the Saginaw River south of Bay City. My father, the oldest, and the first of five brothers to arrive in Saginaw in 1925, helped to bring his four other brothers from Arkansas. He left home at the age of thirteen, traveled and worked around the country and lived in Wyoming, Utah, Nebraska, California, Kansas, Michigan and other points in between. He told me of his experiences working for the railroad and following the work as it arose. This helped me to understand how Blacks and Hispanics found their way to places like Green River, Wyoming; Omaha, Nebraska; Des Moines, Iowa; Kingman, Arizona; Barstow, California and points in between – long before the scholarly mentions of the African-American "Great Migrations."   He moved to Saginaw from Kansas City, Kansas, seeking work, followed by his bride, Flora Martha Nance Bowman and their five-month-old daughter, Evelyn. He was self-educated, became an ordained Minister, an early union organizer, and an International Representative of the United Auto Workers - CIO. He worked hard to provide for his family of eight, which included: two daughters, four sons and a stay-at-home wife.

On November 29, 1934, Thanksgiving day in Saginaw, I imagine that it was cold and probably snowing. That evening at 710 North Franklin Street, I was born in the Bowman home,. My parents, Rev. William S. Bowman Sr. and Flora Martha Nance Bowman, along with their four other children, were celebrating the birth of their fourth and youngest son. Since children were born at home during this era, Evelyn, born in 1926; William Jr., born in 1927; Kenneth born in 1931; and Delano, born in 1933 were somewhere in the home, awaiting for my arrival. Elizabeth Jean, the youngest of my sisters, would follow in October 1936.

When I was growing up, the summers were short, and winters were cold with lots of snow. Used ice skates were cheap at the rummage sales; I bought a pair and learned to skate at a very young age. There were no school buses or snow days. Children had snowsuits that covered them from their neck to their feet. When it snowed, you were dressed in your snowsuit, cap, galoshes, scarf, and mittens, taken outside and if you were able to move through the snow, you went to school. Our school was about a mile and a half away. Teachers would help you get out of your gear and place it on radiators to dry and help you to get back in it for your return home for lunch. The procedure was followed after lunch so that you could finish the day.

In the early days of the automotive industry, General Motors built two large foundries in Saginaw, the Chevrolet Grey Iron Foundry and The Malleable Foundry, which offered employment to many Negroes who were migrating from the South. According to my father, the work was hard, dirty and hazardous. He went to work for General Motors as a molder in 1926 at the Malleable, and then on to the Grey Iron, where work was a little easier. At the beginning of his employment, there was no such thing as an employee union and workers were at the mercy of the company. In 1937, he joined the United Auto Workers Union and served as a committeeman and a member of the Executive Board of local 668 from 1938 until 1940, during a very difficult time of internal strife.

At the time, Rev. Bowman was the Pastor of Christ Community Church and used his influence and union position to have the local hire a Negro female as secretary, where she served until she retired. He served on the UAW International staff as an International Representative from 1940 through 1944 and from 1949 until he retired in 1965. I interviewed my father in 1981 and recorded it on audiotape and again in 1987, which I recorded on a VHS video recorder. In these interviews, I was able to obtain information about my family history and to ask questions that most children are never able to obtain about their family. I have kept copies of these interviews for my children and grandchildren.

Although I was born in the middle of the depression, I recall that my parents always owned more than one house. I have also been told that my mother drove an automobile to Wichita, Kansas, with me in the back window when I was six months old. I remember her owning and driving a 1936 Ford and I assume that it was a family car.

The house at 634 North Franklin Street in Saginaw, Michigan was the first home that I, as a child, can remember. This house sat on the corner of Franklin and Astor and was a large house with a two-car garage facing Astor Street. I remember this house being my first home, although I was born down the street at 710 North Franklin Street, which the family also owned; but I have no recollection of having lived there. The home at 634 N. Franklin Street served as our family home, but I'll always remember it as the house where we also took in roomers. *A roomer is a person that rented a room in another person's house.* I shared a room with my three older brothers. It was not unusual to get up in the night and meet someone that I had never seen before in the hallway. I would find out in the morning that these were new roomers that my mother had taken in during the evening, after I had gone to sleep. Years later, I realized that this house not only served as a home for the family, but it was a refuge for young people who were moving to Saginaw from the South and other parts of the country and the world. Single men, single women and young couples became part of a large extended family.

As a child growing up, I never thought of them as extended family, but rather I saw them as intruders in our home. I vowed never to take in boarders or roomers in my home when I grew up. We were taught to respect these people and to provide support and assistance when they needed it. On occasions we cleaned for them, cooked for them and ran errands for them if they were ill. When my mother told us to "go and see about them", she meant for us to do what they needed. We never questioned it; we just did what we were told. Delano, the brother closest to my age, was the pastor of Bethel A.M.E. Church in Saginaw during the 1990's. Over the years, people often came to him to tell how they rented from our parents, and how they had helped when they first came to the city.

I have many fond memories of my boyhood in Saginaw, Michigan.

Our neighborhood was racially integrated. The house behind us on Astor Street is where my best friend Wally Booshaw lived with his family. Wally was white and he and I played together a lot. I remember we were about the same age and we got along well. We did boy's stuff like running, climbing, playing, and of course, what we thought was training, but what was actually just playing with our dogs. We had a group of five or six other boys that played together. My memories include me being the group leader. I remember going to the dime store and buying some Saint Patrick's Day badges for each one in the group and declaring that we were now a club, and I was their leader. We wore them with pride until we lost them, or they wore out. When one of Wally's young family members from Northern Michigan was visiting and declared, "Look there is a nigger," Wally said, "Where? I don't see one". When the relative pointed to me, Wally said, "No that's Fred." We then resumed our activities with the relative joining us.

When I was not playing or going to school, I worked. Everyone in my family worked. I started kindergarten at age four, yet I remember working before I started school. My children shared the joke about me working my whole life but quit laughing when they saw my Social Security report that showed contributions in the first recorded period of the Social Security program's existence. I remember helping my older brother sweep and clean a beauty school before I even began school. That memory stays with me, as to how hard it is to sweep and mop around human hair. Work wasn't an option in our family; it was an expectation. We were told many times, "You can't live anywhere for free." We worked doing whatever we could and gave part of what we made back to the family. I remember being fired from a job as janitor and shoeshine boy at a downtown barbershop after applying and receiving my Social Security Card. I don't remember how old I was at the time, but they told me that no one my age had applied for a Social Security card and that I needed to find out how to spell my middle name. They would check to see if they could issue me a card. I returned the next day, spelled my middle name for them, and received the card.

My work ethic was okay, but I was told that they thought that I was too young because I bought a small rubber car with some of the tips and was playing with it around the shoeshine stand. I don't recall having many new toys. We learned to make things from whatever we found. A two-by-four, an orange crate, and a single roller skate split in half became a scooter. Four wheels, a box, and a rope became a wagon. We then used the homemade wagon to load two 32-gallon trashcans and pull it across town to the dump, an all-day job that earned about fifty cents split between two brothers.

Mother had a roomer at the house by the name of Sidney, who was also a carpenter; he built a two-chair shoeshine stand. We set it up on the corner of Potter and 4th Street and put some rollers on it so that we could move it off the sidewalk at night. We built a good business. Kenneth was the manager, and Delano and I worked there. We also worked at the grocery store across the corner, selling newspapers and cleaning houses—whatever it took. I learned to repair bicycles and build things early. I don't recall anyone giving me any instructions on using tools until I was in grade school and high school; but I remember repairing and building things long before that. I don't remember ever seeing my father with a hammer or a wrench in his hand, but after I became an adult, he told me that as a young man he had worked in building repair. Before I was eleven years old, I worked at the cleaners in the summer. The owner worked somewhere else, opened it in the morning and closed it in the evening. I took in the clothes, wrote the tickets, tagged the items, sent them out for cleaning and pressing and handled the customer's money. This was in 1944. I am afraid that in today's society, someone would have taken the clothes, the money and possibly me. I also found work in a hardware store on a day in 1945 when the family moved from Saginaw to Detroit. I found myself in trouble because I was holding up the departure when I was completing work that resulted in a couple of bucks.

My Mother was the Head Negro in Charge (H.N.I.C.) in our house. She ruled with an iron fist. No one got big enough to escape her punishment. In today's environment, she would have been sent to jail for child abuse. She would hit us with whatever she had in her hand. One day she discovered that someone had eaten all of the marshmallows that she kept in a large jar. When she confronted Delano and me about it, we quickly confessed. She promptly hit each of us in the head with the jar. When the room quit spinning, I rethought the statement "confession is good for the soul." It may be good for the soul, but it was not good for the head! Her weapons of choice were switches, leather belts and her favorite - an iron's cord.

I know that my mother loved us, but she had experienced a difficult childhood. Her parents died when she was a young child and a cousin who had other children raised her and treated her badly. Mother's story of revenge was about the time that she left the top off of a barrel of molasses and the cat got stuck in it trying to eat some. The barrel top was marked, and mother was told that she had to eat from that barrel. The other family members would eat from another properly marked barrel. Mother changed the top, complained as much as allowed and cried as she ate the clean molasses. The rest of the family finished the cat molasses.

I never knew much about my mother's family other than her two sisters and one brother lived in Saginaw. We were told that mother was born in Muskogee, Oklahoma on May 10, 1899. Her grandmother was American Indian, and her birth records were destroyed in a fire. When the U.S. Army did a background check for my top-secret security clearance, we were told that her birthday was another day in May, but we continued to celebrate it on the tenth anyway.

Mother often reminded us how hard her life had been, and how mean her cousins had been to her. She also said that we needed to work and pay rent to live at home. "You can't live anywhere for free" was her expression. Another phrase that I heard often was "If you don't like it, get out". I didn't like it, but I didn't have anywhere to go, so I stayed until I finished high school at seventeen years old. We were told there was little or no money for new clothes, toys, or other things that kids want. We were taken to rummage sales and thrift stores for shoes and clothing. I was an adult before I realized that we actually were not poor when I was growing up. Years later my oldest sister, Evelyn, told me that she had also figured out that we had been misled to believe we were poor during our childhood.

Growing up, I was curious about many things. I asked many questions about many things. I wanted to know about life …other places, other people and religions. Children weren't supposed to ask too many questions when I was young. You were told to shut up, sit down, do what you were told, and you had better do just that! My mother believed that all money that was earned should come through her._She would then give you back some of *your* money to spend. Generally, I went along with the program, but often I was defiant. I thought that I should be able to spend some of the money, a penny or two for a soda, before I came home. Wrong answer! Do it again and get a beating. I did, I got a beating. I did it again, the same result. We went through the switch, belt and the ironing cord._We then started on beatings in a dark room because I would run from her. The beating went further to a dark room with the ironing cord with me being naked. Think about running around a dark room naked while trying to protect your eyes and your family jewels at the same time.

I didn't want to comply completely about the money, so I devised a plan that allowed me to use some of my earnings and bring home the full amount. When we sold newspapers and we worked the bars. People who are drinking don't want to be bothered by kids, and they don't need newspapers. If you try hard to sell them the paper they will pay for the paper and let you keep it. Then you sell it again and you have money for a treat. When not selling newspapers, we would work the bars and the streets soliciting money to establish a club to keep "kids like us" off the streets. No, it wasn't honest, but it sure beat the ironing cord dance!

As I grew older, I was able to make enough money so that I had some money left after I paid my rent. Life got better, fewer beatings. I had another problem for which I couldn't come up with a solution. I was a bed-wetter, and my mother didn't believe that I couldn't correct it. I tried everything that I could think of, but some nights I would wet the bed. There were nights I spent in the bathroom on the toilet; other times I tried to stay awake all night. When I awoke and found that I had had another accident, I would do whatever I could to keep her from finding out. I would hide the bedding, wash the bedding during the night, change the sheets and/or make up the wet bed. Most times, I received some physical punishment when the truth was discovered. I had a problem with this into my teens, but I was never given a physical to see if it was a medical problem.

No one was too big for my mother to hit. My oldest brother William Jr., six years my senior at twenty, was still living at home. He started drinking. He never learned to drink responsibly. When he came home under the influence, mother would beat him. He was an alcoholic from the beginning and couldn't help himself. He was treated as if he was defiant and didn't care. It was many years later that he found help through Alcoholics Anonymous and quit drinking. Before this, he had been in many auto accidents, one of which almost cost him his life. He lost employment and had two failed marriages. William's heart was as big as Australia. He worked hard, wrote poetry, loved people, was remarried, never had children of his own, but raised over a dozen of other people's children's before he made his transition in 2000.

In 1940, my father went to work for the UAW as an International Representative in Detroit. He was later sent to Buffalo, New York. He came home on some weekends, but mother was in charge and did most of the parenting. Mother provided the guidance, love, encouragement and direction. From her I learned to be caring, helpful, compassionate, entertaining, to work hard, and to be grateful and trust God. I loved my mother and tried to show that love by returning home, as often as possible. from wherever I lived or traveled, and by assuring her that she had whatever she needed or wanted. I tried to always be there for her if she needed me. She did an excellent job. None of my siblings ever got into serious trouble.

We did not live in the 2nd Ward, where many of the colored people lived. Our house was on the other side of the tracks (two or three blocks). My father also owned at least one house and a lot in the 2nd Ward. There was a community center where we would go and play games and where there were more black children. Delano and I would sell most of our newspapers from "The Kansas City Call," a colored paper there. The railroad tracks that separated the 2nd Ward from us had four or more sets of tracks crossing Washington Street. One day after a hard rain, Kenneth who was 3 1/2 years older than I, the third oldest brother, Delano and I were crossing the tracks. It was warm and cars had no air conditioning at the time. Kenneth found a woman's fur choker lying in the roadway that was full of water. He playfully picked it up, swung it around his head several times and let it go. A car that was also crossing the tracks at the same time had the windows down and the wet choker went through the side window and into the face of the woman passenger. They thought that he did it on purpose and the chase was on, they in the car and we on foot. They had the speed, but we had the quick turn-around. After several U-turns, we made a quick break; we made it back home and had our laugh for the week.

Potter Street was in a small business area a few blocks from our house, and it ran parallel to the railroad tracks. Delano and I were walking along Potter Street when I was about six. I discovered a large whiskey bottle. Before I could throw it in the trash, Delano, eighteen months older, told me to take it into the bar in front of where we were standing and get the deposit for it. I was young, and had taken soda and milk bottles for deposit, but never a whiskey bottle. He knew better, because he had often talked me into trouble before and after this happened. When I asked the bartender for the deposit, he told me there was none and to get out.

People who drink sometimes feel good and they show it. A patron said for me to wait and asked me how I would use the money. I saw a large Hershey Bar behind the bar and said I wanted it. He had the bartender give it to me. When I returned with the candy, Delano, who had expected to see me get tossed out, claimed the largest part because he had told me to take it in. On another occasion, while playing in the basement, Delano provided me with some matches and dared me to light a couch that was then stuffed with straw. I lit it and it quickly blazed up. "What do we do now?" I asked. "Let's go upstairs and close the door," he replied. Evelyn, who is my oldest sister, was then about fourteen, and is now a retired schoolteacher and mother of seven children.

When the smoke came up the vents, she ran down and saw the fire. She grabbed every large bucket and pot that she could find, filled them with water and put them on the stove to heat. When she thought the water was hot, she ran down and threw it on the fire. There is a God. Mother came home soon before things got out of hand totally. She turned on the hose attached in the basement and put out the fire. Yes! Big time ironing cord dance! First, we went a few rounds with mother and then daddy provided the final parental punishment when he came home. Evelyn was happy to hear that a fire could be put out with cold water.

There was a wooded area near our house called PM Woods. In the summer, we would hike, run and play in the woods. My brothers let me try my first cigarette there. I may have even tried my first cigar there, which I came to enjoy and continued to smoke until I was over sixty. Our youngest sister was Elizabeth Jean, only eighteen months younger than I, but always thought of as my little sister. She is the only family member that I can recall not working as a child. Our mother would take us to the park for picnics. Every Sunday we went to church, sometimes several times. We would visit my mother's sisters, Aunt Mabel, who lived on a farm, and Aunt Fannie, who lived in the city. Nether of the sisters had children of their own. Aunt Mabel adopted a boy and a girl. It was on her farm that I learned that I didn't like milk after I saw it come out of the cow, not having seen liquid coming from any other part of the cow. No eggs for me either, after I saw the chicken get up off of them. It took years before I relented and started to eat eggs and drink milk. Oh yes, and a few visits from the belt or ironing cord.

Among my fondest memories of the farm was when Delano took Kenneth's new cap and threw it into the pigpen. The pigs couldn't wear it, but they sure had a ball tearing it into small pieces. Back in the city I mistakenly called Aunt Fannie's husband "Buster" during a visit. Following one of their arguments, she told me that "Buster" was the dog's name, but that her husband was nothing but a dog anyway.

My father had four brothers in Saginaw. Bumpkin had a daughter; Thaddeus had a son. Alvin and Eugene also had children. My dad's only living sister was Aunt Emma, who had two children. Anthony was about my age, and Marceline was about twenty years younger than I. We spent more time with Evelyn, Uncle Bumpkin's daughter, and Samuel, Uncle Thaddeus's son, than with the other cousins because they were the only children. Samuel and his family lived on the north edge of town towards Bay City. There were picnic areas along the Saginaw River where families would picnic and fish. Mother had taken us there often.

One summer day, Kenneth, Delano, Samuel, Evelyn and I walked about five miles from Samuel's house to a picnic area along the river. We played and ate our lunch before someone said it would be nice to do some fishing. We didn't have anything to fish with, but Samuel said he would take care of that. He left and returned a short time later with several poles and some worms. We began fishing, but before we caught anything, we saw what looked like an angry white lynch mob coming towards us. They surrounded us, except for Evelyn who took off in a dead run, headed for Samuel's house. The people accused us of beating up some kids and taking their fishing gear. We didn't know where the items came from but knew that most of us had done nothing wrong. More white people arrived, and they were about to take us away when Uncle Bumpkin, his wife and some other adults from the family arrived. The adults were able to sort things out, after Samuel admitted that he had taken the items from the kids and didn't tell us. We were glad to get back to the house, but sorry that we weren't able to list Evelyn's time in the Guinness World Records Book for the fastest time ever recorded for her sprint back to bring adult help.

On another occasion, Delano used his gift of persuasion to get Kenneth to jump from the high end of the garage. Kenneth always liked money and Delano promised him fifty cents if he jumped. None of us had ever tried this stunt before, but for a half dollar, Kenneth was willing to try. Lying on the ground in pain following his historic jump, he asked for his money, only to be told by Delano that he didn't have it. His legs hurt too much to chase Delano, who was laughing as he ran back into the house.

Growing up with three older brothers was fun, exciting, and filled with memories. One of the older brothers, believed to be

Kenneth. slid down a telephone pole. Many splinters later, no one else ever tried it again. We played games that required little, if any, equipment. Games were made up to use the items that we had. I remember "Mad Dog." We tied a rope around the waist of a kid, and he was Mad Dog. Everyone would tease him and let him chase us as far as the rope would allow. When someone got too close and was caught, they became Mad Dog. This was a great game, unless mother's clothesline was used and it broke. Yes, we got our butts beat.

If we found an auto hub cap (wheel cover now) we would walk around with it as if it were a steering wheel, make motor sounds, hit the center and make horn noises while entertaining ourselves. I remember the iceman, the coal man, the junk man, and the milkman; all delivering with horses and then changing to trucks. We collected tin cans and then cleaned and flattened them and used them for admission to the theatre during the war drives. At the end of World War II, V-J Day, May 8, 1945, I was 10-years-old and we went to downtown Saginaw to celebrate.

Evelyn and William Jr. had already graduated from high school, and when school was out for the summer in 1945, we packed the family into a two-car caravan and moved to Detroit, Michigan, our new home. I am the only sibling in the family who has moved from Michigan, except for Kenneth who went to Wilberforce University, prior to his death.

CHAPTER 2

CALL ON A SPECIALIST

As morning broke over the room and the dim light from the open blinds glared in over the hospital bed, a nurse very gently nudged me and said. "Wake up Fred. It's morning." As my eyes opened, it was difficult for me to conceive being in a hospital bed. A light from a small lamp gave me a sensation, such as one that might be felt by a delirious sailor adrift in a small raft on a high sea. The next thing I remember was the nurse placing a thermometer in my mouth, as she bid me good morning. she asked me if there was feeling in those limbs that were paralyzed; I believe that this was my *first* real awakening, due to the fact that most of the limbs of my body were completely immobilized.

As I lay in that hospital bed, my mind drifted back to that Sunday morning when I had awakened with plans of attending a civil rights rally in Saginaw, Michigan with my brother Kenneth, who was then Chairman of the State NAACP Youth Conference. Kenneth and I had been a team, along with Delano, another older brother, who was then Chairman of the Detroit chapter of the NAACP Council. It had been customary for us to travel in a group throughout the State of Michigan, addressing groups of people, who were interested in the civil rights movement. This Sunday was no different than many others, in that we had planned to attend an afternoon rally in Saginaw, Michigan. I had been appointed Chairman of the speaker's bureau of the State Conference of the NAACP Youth and had prepared myself to speak on subjects pertinent to the civil rights movement.

That morning as I awoke, after being called by Kenneth, I left the bed and entered the bathroom on the third floor of my mother's home. For the first time in my life, I felt faint, then I experienced a sensation of dizziness, and I thought perhaps it was from lack of rest. Kenneth and I had often laughed together about being superhuman individuals, persons who were able to withstand more pressure and do without more rest than the average person; so for a moment, as the room spun around me, I wondered if our little joke had fallen through. I made my way, back to bed in the hopes of gaining more strength and going about my normal tasks. It was approximately one and a half hours later, when Kenneth called a second time, asking me if I was still going with him to Saginaw that I decided to make a second attempt at getting up and dressing. Once again, I went into the bathroom; but once again, the dizziness returned and this time I passed out. Kenneth came up and found me/ He helped me back to bed, and I explained to him that I thought I would be okay if only I could get a couple hours more sleep.

It was only a few minutes later that my mother entered the room and asked me if I was okay and if I wanted her to call the family doctor. I told her that I would be all right, that it was just lack of sleep and over-indulging in schoolwork and club activities. I told her, "If I'm left alone, I'll snap out of it." With this assurance, she went about her chores and I returned to sleep for a couple hours more. Upon attempting the third time to get up and dress, I had finally come to the realization that there was something physically wrong with me and that perhaps it was necessary to see a physician. I called my mother and explained to her how I felt and asked her to call a doctor.

The family doctor arrived, and after a very brief examination, he told my mother that I was running a very high temperature and he was afraid I had the flu. I remember mother asking me why I hadn't told her that I was this sick, and I replied that I actually wasn't aware that I was really this sick. After administrating to what he then believed was my illness, I was given medication and the doctor left. Later on that night, I felt much worse and the doctor was called back to check on my condition. When he returned the second time, the doctor said that he felt my illness was more than the flu and perhaps pneumonia. My mother was told that in the morning I should be admitted to the hospital.

By morning, my condition hadn't improved. A further diagnosis, although they didn't tell me, was that I was coming down with Polio. An ambulance was called to take me to Herman Keefer Hospital in Detroit. I was very aware that this hospital is the center for polio cases and tuberculosis. I'll never forget the thoughts that passed through my mind that morning, when the ambulance crew climbed to the third floor with their stretcher and carefully placed me on it; it was January 1953 and quite cold. They were very particular in that they made very sure I was wrapped and covered warmly. As they carried me down the front steps and out the door, the sensation of fear passed through my mind -- the fear that one gets when he might possibly know that he is dying or that he is making a trip from which he will never return.

The ambulance moved very slowly, and as I lay there, I was overcome with a feeling one might experience being carried in a hearse on his way to the cemetery; if it were possible to acknowledge such a feeling. Without any reservation, I'll admit, I was scared. We arrived at Herman Keefer Hospital that afternoon and we were processed very quickly. I was taken to a room and told that they were going to give me a spinal tap. They didn't tell me that they thought I had Polio, but by that time I was very aware of their suspicions. I have had many pains in my life, but none I recall being quite as painful as this spinal tap. I remember so distinctly they doubled my body over and with several very capable assistants, they held me tightly as the spinal tap was made. After lab tests, they told my mother that the reports were negative and that there were no indications of polio in my body.

A second ambulance was called, and I was removed from Herman Keefer to a small hospital called Martin Place. As the attendants there carried me in on a stretcher to my room, my mind began to wander and I thought to myself that as a freshman student at the University of Detroit, unable to cope with the worries of making the payment on the tuition., buy books etc., *I thought I had problems.* However, now my problems had generated greater momentum and had reached a point that I had never imagined. Now everything was completely out of orbit, for I had little control over my limbs, and I lay completely helpless on a hospital stretcher, being taken to a hospital bed in hopes that they could diagnose my condition and restore unity and strength to my body.

I remember them rolling me into the hospital room and the attending nurse putting me to bed and asking me if I had any control over my body at all. Although my speech and my senses were not impaired, I felt completely helpless, because this was the first time in my life that I had actually been seriously sick. I lay in the hospital room gazing at the ceiling, trying to evaluate how sick I really was, and wondering if I ever would regain full use of my body again. Although I wasn't completely afraid, in the back of my mind, I felt a sense of fear -- fear for those many dreams that I had hoped and prayed for...dreams of growing up in a new society -- a society of love, goodwill and understanding. My dream was of accomplishment…it was a dream of being strong, healthy and of contributing. Now I feared that instead of being a builder, I was to be a burden.

As the nurse re-entered the room to remove the thermometer and read it, her voice returned me from my deep thoughts. She recorded the reading on my chart and left. It was then that I realized I was not in the room by myself, that this was not a private room, but a semi-private one. Upon looking around, I discovered that there was another man in the room with me, occupying another bed. Much to my surprise, he appeared quite jovial and inquired as to the nature of my illness. I explained to him that it hadn't been diagnosed completely yet, but that I was afraid of possible Polio. He smiled and added that I shouldn't worry until it was completely diagnosed.

The next morning after breakfast, a specialist arrived, gave me a thorough physical, and with the assistance of electrocardiograph and several other devices, be diagnosed that I was suffering from an attack of rheumatic fever and that my heart had been affected by the attack. After the extensive tests were over, I returned to the hospital room and my roommate again asked as to the nature of my illness. I explained to him that the doctor said it was rheumatic fever and that complete recovery was nil and that I would be an invalid for the rest of my life.

My roommate then looked directly at me and said, "Do you believe in God?" I, of course assured him that I did. He then said to me:

> *When I entered this hospital, it was with my third occurrence of double pneumonia. Actually, I wasn't told because I was too ill, but my family was informed that I was suffering from double pneumonia and that death was imminent and complete recovery was an impossibility. They doctored over me for several hours with all the modern devices that were at their disposal, but my condition appeared to be hopeless. Therefore, I was abandoned and left at the mercy of God. I realized, after the door was closed and the doctors left, that now it was time to call a real specialist -- It was then that I called on Christ. There was little doubt in my mind and very little apprehension, for I realized that He was the greatest of doctors and that the Master who had created life, surely could heal my body. I called on Him, a specialist of specialists, and reminded Him that mine was a stricken body and that I was asking Him to oversee the doctors and to help me in my recovery.*

My roommate told me that the doctors were completely amazed upon re-examination that the body that they had given up for lost, the body that they had diagnosed "hopeless" the condition for which they didn't conceive any chance of recovery, showed signs of complete recovery. He told me that if I had the faith and if I believed, and that if I applied myself, I could regain control of my body. He told me that the Chief of Specialists, who he had called on, was not only a specialist with regard to pneumonia, but also a specialist for all illnesses, both physical and mental. However, these doctors, he said could only cure those who believed, those who would call on Him, had the faith, and believed within themselves.

It didn't take me very long to realize that if I had the faith and believed and called on the Master, that my body too could be restored so that once again I could live a full life. I lost no time calling on Him – and I did so with a deep, sincere faith that He would help me. It was amazing - relief was not a long way off, for after a short time my fingers began to move, and I was able to bend my elbows and raise my arms. Though slightly painful, my legs began to move, and my joints began to feel life again. I knew that the specialist that I had called on had begun to work on my body, also. much to the surprise of the hospital personnel, I had left the hospital bed and was out in the corridor within a short time. I was standing on the scale weighing myself to see how much weight I had lost during my illness, when one of the nurses approached and told me that I should be in bed. And I could tell by the startled expression on her face that she was also surprised at my miraculous recovery. Upon her demand, I returned to my room and uttered a prayer for the blessing I had received. After being shown a cardiogram and other reports from doctors and specialists, I was told that, although I had regained the use of my body again, I would still be an invalid for the remainder of my life and that my activities would be limited.

Realizing that surely the divine Specialist could restore movement to the body could certainly maintain this movement and strengthen it-- I called on the Specialist, once again.

Contrary to the advice of doctors, who had warned me that I should not take part in anything strenuous, I now recall many activities not within the limits of an invalid. I recall that I moved to Cleveland, Ohio in 1953 and took a job as a laborer in the Steel Mills. I remember entering the U.S. Army in 1954 and completing Basic Training, while competing in all of the physical activity required of a recruit. I remember the vigorous activity demanded of us Candidates in Infantry Officers Candidate School. I remember so many times on long runs, when my companions were passing out and falling by the wayside, that the Chief Specialist revived this body and made it capable of continuing to run when others failed. In addition, having had four and a half years of military service behind a very active life, I recall many occasions when this body should have faltered. Being the father of three very spry and frisky young children, I am often called upon by them for advice and assistance, when they are in difficulty. When I tell them that they must do certain things they tell me, "Daddy, I can't", I only smile and think of the great Specialist, who makes all things possible. I would tell them, "when you believe, and you have faith, and you apply yourself, have faith, try, and you can do anything!"

From the life of Frederick E. Bowman, written in 1966, about my bout with Rheumatic Fever in December 1952 and into 1953 when I was eighteen. It was never published or distributed.

CHAPTER 3

LEAVING HOME
FOR THE FIRST TIME

On an early Sunday morning, August 30, 1953, I was eighteen years old. I had awakened early and had finished my breakfast. This was a very important day in my life, and I wanted it to get off to a good start. I had decided that this would be the day that I would leave home for the very first time. I had not told any other member of my family about my plans to leave home. In fact, I was not sure that this was something that I would actually go through with.

My mother came into the kitchen and asked me if I had enjoyed the party that I had the night before. I had enjoyed a good time with several of my friends. I had not even revealed to anyone my plan to leave Detroit. However, I would use this opportunity, with my father out of town, to make a move to Cleveland, Ohio, to look for a job. My mother was upset when I told her that I was leaving and said that I couldn't leave while my father was out of town. She often told the children, "If you don't like what is going on here, you can get out" and I told her that I was leaving. I knew nothing about Cleveland,

Ohio, at this time except where it was on the map. I knew that the auto industry dictated the number and type of jobs available in and around Detroit. I don't recall how much money I had at that time, but I would guess that it was substantially less than $100. I knew where the Greyhound bus station was in downtown Detroit, so I took a city bus down to the station and purchased a one-way ticket to Cleveland. The bus ride was about four hours, not very exciting. I arrived in the early afternoon.

After walking around downtown Cleveland for a while, I found my way to 79th Street and Cedar. There was a Y.M.C.A. on the corner of 76th. The Y.M.C.A was full, and I asked the desk clerk where I could find a room to rent. He referred me to woman by the name of Helen Freeman, who lived on 76th Street. He told me that, on occasion, she had rooms for rent.

When I met Mrs. Helen Freeman that Sunday afternoon, little did I know what an important part she would play in my life. She was a middle-aged woman married to Mr. Robert (Bob) Freeman, and they lived in the rear house on a piece of property where there were two houses, one behind the other. She was a very friendly and pleasant woman who appeared to be surprised that someone my age would be looking for a room to rent. I explained to her that I had come to Cleveland looking for another city that was different from Detroit and wanted to try life on my own for the first time.

The Freemans had one daughter who was a little older than I. She was married and lived somewhere else. They said that they could make room for me at a reasonable rate. The room was small, but I was alone and only had a suitcase and a few other items with me at the time. Mrs. Freeman told me that the room would not be available for another day, so I walked the streets of Cleveland, became tired and got a cheap hotel room for four dollars. On Monday, I started to look for work, leaving applications at several places, but found nothing. On Monday evening, I moved into the room on the second floor, at the rear of the front house.

I spent the next day looking for work, but still found nothing. After a couple of days, my money was running low, so I cut back on meals. I found myself with only twenty-five cents. I thought about pawning my watch and remembered the expression "Man's limitation is God's opportunity" so I bought myself a pack of gum and kept my watch. Upon leaving the store, I noticed a young man looking at me. I walked away and noticed that he appeared to be gay. He followed me for a short distance. I stopped and asked him if he was following me and asked why. He apologized and said that he worked at the Wade Park Manor Hotel and that the manager had asked him to try to find some young men to work as busboys. This wasn't what I was looking for in work, but I changed into my only white shirt and dark pants and began work that night. The wages were very low, but they let the busboys eat all they wanted of most foods. The waiters split their tips with everyone each night. I arrived back at the room late that night, but with a full stomach and $1.00 in tips; more cash than I had earned since I left home. The second day my tips went up to $1.25 and on the third day, because I was working alone, $3.75. The hours at the hotel were long. They required that we be there for breakfast, lunch and dinner. They also worked us seven days a week. After two weeks, I asked when my day off was and they told me they would let me know. The next Saturday I said that I wanted to go to church and was asked "What is more important, the job or going to church?" When I said church, I received my first time off and came to work, following the services. The following week, I told them that I needed a day off. The manager was reluctant but told me to take Monday off.

Early Monday morning I was at the employment office of Republic Steel and was hired after a test and an interview. My test scores were high, and they gave me the job of Foreman's assistant, but the Union raised so much of a storm that they took me out of it after several days. I then became a Dryer Machine Operator. This large machine would fill with wet salt, tumble it until it was dry, empty the salt and then the process was repeated. There was little effort or work; in fact, it was boring and difficult to stay awake. Although I had been warned, I awoke one night with wet salt up to my waist and the room full after a machine shut down while I was asleep. Using very hot water, I washed it all down the sewer. I'm sure that it didn't help the plumbing, but that was my secret. This job lasted for several weeks, after which I became a laborer.

Any type of work in the steel mill is hard work. The place is hot in some areas, cold in others and dirty in all areas. Everything there is heavy. Much of the equipment in the mill is dangerous. When I worked in the Hot Strip Mill, sirens sounded often, which meant that the red, hot steel that was moving through the rollers (which was pressed it into sheet) had jumped the track and was running through the mill employee area. One learned early in his employment to dash for cover or to a safe place. One of the most difficult conditions for me to adjust to was that steel workers worked one-week days, one-week afternoons and one-week midnights. I found myself getting ready for work when I should have been sleeping and vice versa.

A room became available on the first-floor front of the rooming house. I rented it, wall papered it and bought myself a new television set. I hung new drapes and added new bedding. My room became the show place of the rooming house. Living in a rooming house was nothing new to me, as I was raised in one. In Saginaw, Michigan, my parents took in renters in the early years of my life. Often, I would meet someone in the house at night or in the morning that my parents had rented to after I went to bed. The other renters in this house were a unique group of people. There were two other single men, a single woman, a family of four (husband, wife, young son and daughter about thirteen) and me. Everyone in the house was older than I except for the children of the family that lived on the second floor. Everyone had his or her own story and personality. Everyone worked except for one of the men, a senior citizen, who had many stories to tell, most of which were embellished.

On occasion the house would have a Blue Monday Party where some of us would cook up a dish. Drinks were bought and stories, jokes and outright lies were told, rebuffed, disputed, and retold. I was a pretty good cook and had learned early the skill of drinking within my limits. I had also learned to tell a few stories, some true and some otherwise. I looked forward to the Blue Monday parties because I liked people and took every opportunity to learn about life. We shared a refrigerator and I would prepare my lunch and place it in there before going to bed. Several times it was missing when I went to take it to work. I believed that the young boy who lived upstairs was eating it, although he denied it. One morning after it was missing I found him in the kitchen and told him that I had set a trap for the thief. I said that I had poisoned the sandwich. I told in great detail how the poison would slowly work. It would cause the thief to become sleepy, start to cramp and cause death within 10 hours if he didn't get the antidote. I was careful to make it sound as bad as I could and to explain how little time the thief had to take the antidote. He began crying and begging me to get him the antidote. I let him cry for a while and told him that I hadn't poisoned the lunch, but that he didn't know if I would really do it. My lunch was safe after that. I soon learned that although there was no one there to tell me what to do, how late to stay out, where or when to go, I did the right thing because that was what I had been taught and how I was raised. I also learned that when you are responsible for yourself, you had better take care of business and yourself …there is no one else there to do it!

I located an A.M.E. Church near the house and joined. They had an active young people's department and activities that kept me involved. With the Freemans and the other residents in the rooming house, I had a new family.

My mother was concerned about me, since I was the first child - her second to the youngest of six - to leave home, except to get married or go away to college. When I was eighteen, I had left home against her wishes and while under a doctor's care for Rheumatic Fever. I had been paralyzed in the hospital for several weeks. I was on daily medication and had been told in January of that year, that I would be an invalid for the rest of my life with very limited activities. Unbeknownst to mother or anyone else, I had quit taking all medication a few days after arriving in Cleveland. The thought of spending the rest of my life on medication and limited to little or no physical activities didn't appeal to me.

On my own and without anyone to question me or remind me of possible dangers if I were wrong, it allowed me to find out what I could or couldn't do. If the steel mill didn't kill me, maybe other activities would not kill me. After about two months, I invited my mother to visit me in Cleveland. She accepted, without hesitation. Now she could see what I was up to. I took her out to lunch, dinner, church and to a nightclub-- probably her first. We had a great time and she returned to Detroit, believing that I was not killing myself.

When she returned home, I was encouraged to come home, back to Detroit. My parents had several rental properties that I had performed the maintenance work on when I was at home. In addition to missing me, my handyman services were missed.

I continued to work at Republic Steel until being laid off in February 1954. I thought that I could return home and re-enroll at the University of Detroit, where I attended before getting sick. My experiences in Cleveland and my relationship with the Freemans would prove to be very valuable and important in the future. After a short time, following my return to Detroit, I learned that "you can never return home." I now believed that I was physically fit after my experiences in the steel mill.

In early March, I enlisted in the U.S. Army and was sworn in on March 12, 1954.

PART TWO
EMBARKING UPON
NEW TERRITORY

CHAPTER 4

JOINING THE ARMY

Friday, March 12, 1954, I was officially sworn in as a member of the United States Army at the recruitment-processing center in Detroit, Michigan. I was nineteen years old and officially a Private E-2 in the United States Army. We left Detroit in the early morning on Saturday via the railroad for Camp Chaffee, Arkansas. This was just my second time to experience visiting or living in the southern parts of the United States. I was part of a group of recruits traveling on a troop train on an overnight trip, which allowed us to arrive at camp on Sunday, the 14th. I was excited to be with the military and this was my first experience outside of the training that I had received in R.O.T.C. (Reserve Officer Training Corps) in high school and college. I had taken this challenge on with the belief that I could obtain a commission in the United States Army Reserve within one year. I had expressed this intent to my parents before leaving. The only factor that was of concern to me was that I had been less than honest in my application. I failed to include the fact that I had been diagnosed with Rheumatic Fever and had been paralyzed at the age of eighteen. In my mind, I had already overcome this condition and had proven to myself that the doctor's prognosis of being an invalid had been in error. Before joining the Army, I had left home and lived in Cleveland, Ohio, working in the steel mills, lifting steel and heavy objects.

When we arrived at Camp Chaffee, Arkansas, they called for the first formation. They lined everyone up in ranks, as in a platoon. After roll call, the Sergeant in charge called my name, and said I was to report to the orderly room. There was a great deal of concern on my part because I thought the Army had found out either through the physical or an early background check that my application was less then factual.

When I arrived in the orderly room, a representative from the Red Cross told me that he had bad news for me. My brother Kenneth, the second oldest son, third oldest child who was a student at Wilberforce University and a Pastor at Bethel AME church in Saginaw, Michigan, had been in an automobile accident on that Saturday, the day I left Detroit, and he had not survived. The Red Cross said that they would assist me in returning home and the Army gave me an emergency leave. I left Camp Chaffee on a regular service highway bus bound for Detroit that Sunday evening. The trip was one of the longest in my life and was a unique experience for me because at that time, no coloreds were allowed to ride in the front of the bus. In order to ride, I had to sit in the back of the bus, which was not air-conditioned. An elderly lady was sitting in front of me using 'snuff', a form of tobacco, and was spitting out the window, which blew back into my face. When the bus stopped at station spots enroute, the only facilities we were able to use were the ones that said "colored." Those restrooms were inferior and maintained worse than those labeled for "white" passengers.

I arrived home in Detroit to a grieving family. I spent my leave going through the process and helped to prepare the funeral for my brother Kenneth R. Bowman. There were two services held for him: one in Detroit, where he was best known and raised, and one in Saginaw, Michigan, where he was the Pastor of the AME Church. Kenneth had died in a head-on accident in route from Detroit to Saginaw, Michigan, which was a two-lane highway at that time. It was difficult for me to accept that the accident had happened on that highway, since I had driven it and the family had traveled many times on that highway since moving from Saginaw in 1945. We had traveled that highway many times and it was a safe route. Both people in the other car, a husband and wife were also killed. They left children behind. In addition, in Kenneth's car was a young minister who was attending Wilberforce and was traveling along with Kenneth to Saginaw. He was also killed. Our cousin, who had just been released from the service, was traveling in the back seat. He was the only survivor.

Following the funeral, I returned to Camp Chaffee via the bus. That trip wasn't as bad as the trip coming home. I was looking forward to my career in the United States Army. The group I came in with had already started their training, so I was put in a holding unit until the next group was to start, about twenty-eight days from the time the original class began. I took both basic and advanced basic training at Camp Chaffee. The first basic training course was in basic infantry, equipment procedures and weapons. Then I proceeded to the advanced course, which was in Armor and involved 105-millimeter howitzers.

In the first basic training formation, I watched as First Sergeant began to give instructions to the new recruits on military formations, marching steps, and manual of arms. I understood and had both learned and instructed these techniques from past training in high school and college R.O.T.C., but I knew not to reveal my knowledge beforehand. Realizing from viewing the Sergeant's attempt to instruct, I knew that would definitely be to my advantage. There were reserve Non-Commissioned-Officers, as well as reserve-enlisted people in our formation.

After four or five hours, the Sergeant asked someone to step forward and demonstrate, and I volunteered. Performing the following correct procedures he was trying to teach, the First Sergeant then asked me where I learned the procedures, and I informed him "through R.O.T.C.". He then questioned me as to how much I knew. I informed him that I understood the entire manual of arms, as well as other military movements. He then questioned whether I knew them enough to instruct, and I told him that I did. He then asked me to instruct the new recruits in the manual of arms, which I did for the remainder of that day. Within a two-day period, the Sergeant made me the primary instructor and gave me temporary stripes. I found myself in an awkward position being in charge of a unit with people who outranked me.

Upon completion of a battery of tests directed to new recruits, I applied for officer's candidate school. My application was processed while I was acting as an N.C.O. (Non-Commissioned Officer). That gave me an advantage. Most of the people in my unit realized that I had prior military training. It wasn't a surprise to them that I was a candidate for Officer's Candidate School. Prior to the completion of my advanced basic military training, a team of officers interviewed me. The post commanding general told that me that I had been recommended for Officers' Candidate School at Fort Benning, Georgia.

Being that I was an acting Sergeant, some of the people under me thought there was a need to test my authority. The first major incident involved them obtaining the services of a recruit by the name of Zake, a big redneck from one of the southern states who spent all of his spare time lifting weights and bodybuilding. They convinced Zake that I was a menace to the unit, that I had exceeded my authority and ability and that he should inflict physical damage on me. To their delight, Zake approached me one evening when I was sitting on my footlocker cleaning a disassembled carbine. Zake stood there, standing in front of me telling me that "he was going to tear me from limb- to-limb, and I had no authority over anybody there and everyone was tired of taking orders from me." Earlier that day, I had assigned Zake and a group of other recruits to service in the mess hall and they hadn't shown up. I had to reassign other people to that work.

With Zake standing over me, making all of his threats, I refused to make eye contact, but I quickly reassembled my carbine. I was an expert at that, and it only took me a matter of a minute or two. I then placed the weapon on my hip and adjusted the sling and made first eye contact with Zake by saying, "excuse-me" as I stood up. Zake stood back two-steps. I stood up and placed the butt of the carbine alongside of his skull. I then explained to him that if he ever made threats to me or anybody else in the unit, I intended to beat his brains out. I further told him that he would do exactly what I told him to do, when I told him to do it, and not ask any questions. I slapped him upside his head a couple of times, and then asked him if he wanted me to really beat his brains out right then! And if not, he needed to remove himself from my sight! Zake turned and left abruptly. I then announced to the platoon that was waiting to see me get beat up that I was sending the whole unit down to the motor pool to wash Jeeps for the rest of the evening, which I did. I had no trouble from Zake or anyone after that.

There was a second incident toward the end of basic training after we had finished our training and were waiting for reassignment. I was going to Officers' Candidate School (O.C.S.), and the others were headed for Korea. I went to the movies that evening. When I returned I learned several people in the unit were badly beaten. The soldiers who weren't beaten up were somewhere hiding in wall lockers, under beds, and anywhere else that they could find to hide. I was told that a recruit by the name of Allen, a very large and well-developed black recruit who had been a professional boxer had drunk too much and gone crazy. I took an entrenching tool – a folding steel shovel is what it really was. I placed it on top off the wall locker near the entrance to the platoon and went looking for Allen. I was in good physical shape, a very fast runner and believed that I could beat Allen back to the point of the entrenching tool. Once I found him, some distance from the barracks, he was still in a rage. I could tell that his bloody fist and thumb were busted.

Allen had a recruit pinned against the wall. He showed little respect when I called out to him. He responded by saying, "One minute." Then he knocked the recruit out. Once I was upon him, he grabbed me disrespectfully at the collar, drawing his bloody fist back to hit me. I maintained my cool and asked. "Do you know who I am?" The fact that I maintained my cool against such a large man was startling enough to him. With me looking him directly in his eyes, he managed to answer me. "Yes, you're 'Acting Sergeant Bowman'." In the heat of his rage, I continued. "Do you know if you hit me, I plan to kill you?" "What?" was his only reply. I now had his undivided attention. I repeated. "When you hit me, I'm going to kill you." He then stopped, and I told him, "I'm taking you back to the barracks, to wrap your hand." He was under the impression that I was going to call the MP's (Military Police). "I assure you, I won't," I explained to him. "Not unless you make it necessary."

I took Allen back to the barracks and sat him in the restroom, while I went to get a first-aid kit. When I returned, he was sitting in the bathroom laughing hysterically and the entire bathroom window frame and all was out. When I took a look out the open space, I saw a recruit lying on the ground knocked-out. I wrapped up recruit Allen's hand and put him in the bed as others attended to the unconscious recruit. In addition, when I went to assist the other recruits who were injured, I found out ten or eleven recruits were injured and sent to the base hospital.

The unit First Sergeant, who was the Duty Sergeant on the base, approached me later that evening. He had received a report that evening that a member of the unit was being rushed to the hospital. When he approached me, he had his 45-caliber pistol drawn and in a demanding manner asked. "What the hell is going on?" In an appropriate manner, I answered. "I have been to the theater and I wasn't sure what was going on." However, there was a lot of blood, and there was a trail… a trail leading to recruit Allen. He placed the 45 under Allen's nose and demanded that he get up. The Sergeant arrested him and took him to the brig. I had no further contact with recruit Allen. I left for O.C.S. shortly after that. I received a report later that Allen had 'went-off' again like that in Korea. The Army had made claims that they were integrated at that time. Nevertheless, the southern states weren't.

Five of us, by name, received orders. I was one of them, the only one who was colored. We had orders to leave Camp Chaffee. We were to travel by train to Fort Benning. That's when I was told, upon boarding the train, that I had to ride in the car for coloreds. When it came time to eat, we all had one voucher, but we all couldn't sit and eat together. I couldn't eat in the white's area, and the colored restaurant was afraid to have the white recruits in their establishments. We pooled our money and ate where we could. In Memphis, Tennessee, a police officer pulled his gun on me and threatened to shoot me because I was in the white section of the train depot. That was a very miserable trip and about the time I arrived, I was sore at the United States and the Government's Army.

My first experience with Officers' Candidate School caused me to recall all the films and other detail information that I learned about O.C.S. during my high school and college years. Still, I realized very soon that I wasn't ready for what I was about to undergo in this type of training. During the Jeep ride from the train, the enlisted driver said, "So you are going to O.C.S.? Well, they are waiting for you," and he laughed. "Yes, they are waiting for you." When the Jeep stopped in the O.C.S. section of the Fort, I saw some of the hardest, meanest looking soldiers that I had ever seen. The officer candidates had blue loops on their epaulets. I soon found out that they were Senior Officer Candidates that had the power to command and direct junior candidates, such as me. They immediately began to give us instructions, directions and orders. The treatment that I received was horrendous and extreme. It was all day and all night. What transpired - the torment, my first ordeal, my first experience - was literally hell.

My first contact rendered me totally unprepared. I arrived wearing a garrison hat, which has an embedded frame. I didn't pack it with everything else, fearing damage to the blocked shape, so I wore it as a form of protection. This hat, which only one per soldier is issued, is the hat that is worn to the most important events and such affairs as honor parades, and formal dress parades. My first experience happened when I went to register. I encountered a second lieutenant, that in a rude manner immediately asked, "What are you doing with that flying saucer on your head?" My response was totally appropriate, but inadequate to satisfy him. He proceeded to dress me down as I stood at attention. With every answer I gave, his harassment continued with assigned push-ups in groups of tens and twenties. When push-ups weren't ordered, pull-ups were demanded. It was well into the dark hours and the Lieutenant and I, still outside, continued to work me over. I had checked into O.C.S. early in the day, but that didn't matter to this Lieutenant, and I continued to do push-ups.

Most of the candidates had been given bunk, room assignments, and were well on their way to setting-up their uniform displays. We also were given homework assignments. When I was finally released, I made my way to the bed. It was late and I was behind schedule. I remember asking myself: "How did I get into this mess? I'm not sure how I'm going to get out of here." I needed to get out of there because that wasn't a place for me. Somehow, late that evening, I got my uniform display set up and completed the next morning's homework, using a flashlight under a blanket.

Early the next morning, the same Lieutenant, who we found out was our platoon tactical officer, met us. He was assigned to evaluate and determine if we were qualified to become officers of the United States Army. Late into last night, I had already come to the conclusion that the Lieutenant had already done everything that he could do to convince me to want to leave. I further determined that there were only three ways to get out of O.C.S: Fail the course, get out because of physical conditions or graduate. I immediately set my mind on the scheduled completion date, which was March 22, 1955. I had decided that the honorable way was the route I would take to get out of O.C.S. The pressure and the harassment were unbelievable. Candidates would awaken in the night to find our tactical officer standing over their beds watching them sleep, while others would awaken screaming from nightmares.

Our tactical officer had an office on the second floor. During the fifth week, on the first floor, there was a discussion of the large number of demerits that members of the platoon had received from the tactical officer. When it was my turn, I responded, "I have none." The group was in disbelief, since they were given demerits for any and all possible misdeeds. Within minutes we heard, "Bowman, report up here!" in a thundering voice from the tactical officer. I ran up the stairs, because in the first 18 weeks all movement was at double-time. Candidates never walked. After I saluted, I was given six demerits for various things. He had the barracks bugged, because no one had hearing that good, except my mother. In the twelfth week, I received instructions to report to the tactical officer, who offered me a seat (not usually done with candidates). I spoke, "Sir, Candidate Bowman, and no thanks, sir".

"Sit down Bowman," he said. "This discussion never took place," the Lieutenant said. "I have been able to get into everyone's head in the unit; to run off many who I thought weren't qualified. I've intimidated most of the candidates who are here, so why don't you appear to be bothered?"

I replied, "Overkill." "That first day you did everything to me that you could think of; here was nothing left to be afraid of."

When candidates were washed out, or removed, they would disappear. Their area would be cleared out and their names would be removed from all rosters. The cubicles in the barracks were designed for two people. We had four people assigned to each cubicle. Before graduations, there was only one person to each cubicle and some other cubicles were completely empty. The class started with over two hundred candidates and we graduated with ninety-two, which was a very large class and above normal. On March 22, 1955, I participated in the class graduation ceremony and was commissioned Second Lieutenant in the United States Army Reserve. It was one year and ten days after my enlistment.

My youngest sister came to Georgia for my graduation and we planned to return to Detroit via bus. A fellow lieutenant that had been in the school with me was driving back and offered to take us for a reasonable fee. I thought that I knew him and that he had some character, since he had been through the same training and evaluations that I had. Shortly after we were on the road, he stopped at a store and made a purchase, which I later found out, was liquor. He began to drink and continued to drive, over our objections and offers to drive. The trip took a turn for the worst, when I thought that I would have to fight him before we were able to have him drop us in a city where we could catch a bus to Detroit. This was an important lesson: you never know people, regardless of how they may have presented themselves earlier.

CHAPTER 5

SALZBURG, AUSTRIA

After a short leave following O.C.S., I was assigned to travel overseas to Salzburg, Austria. My military occupational specialty, at the time, was Infantry Platoon Leader. Upon my arrival in Salzburg, Austria, I was assigned to the headquarters company, which consists of service groups. My first assignment in the U.S. Army was as a mess officer, for which I was trained, but was not my specialty. Also, I ended up as a motor officer – for this I was also trained, but again, not my specialty. I knew shortly after I arrived in Salzburg, Austria, that my stay there would be for a very short period.

I, along with several other officers, was assigned to a Bachelor Officer Quarters, which also had our own officers' club. Recreational activities in Austria included eating, drinking, playing pool, cards and sleeping. The local female population chose not to associate themselves with U.S. Army personnel and I can't recall any incidents while I was there, where any local woman or U.S. personnel was seen dating a colored enlisted person or Officer of the U.S. Army.

I was assigned to the motor pool, where there were large amounts of equipment. Since this was the Headquarters Company, the motor pool itself consisted of approximately one hundred and fifty vehicles and included in this huge collection of military vehicles were three new unmarked Chevrolet sedans. There were tools, supplies and other valuable equipment that was worth probably millions of dollars. A Motor-Pool Officer has total responsibility over all items in his motor pool. I was the current officer to take over the property book and its full responsibility. I realized that this was more responsibility than I needed to take in any short period.

Being from 'the motor-city' Detroit, street smarts made me somewhat of a natural. I immediately made the right type of friends with the Non-Commission Officers in the motor pool. The Motor Officer, at that time, was in a hurry to transfer the equipment over to me so that he could leave. I don't recall his name, but he was senior in rank, maybe a Captain. He would go to the motor pool, inventory all the equipment and ready it for transfer, along with a scheduled inventory time. I made it a point to make some of the equipment disappear before the schedule inventory time on each occasion. I would have one of the non-commissioned officers to load a deuce and a half ($\frac{1}{2}\frac{1}{2}$ $2\frac{1}{2}$- ton truck) with certain supplies, keeping vehicles out on road tests for that certain period during inventory.

The Motor-Pool Captain was extremely frustrated trying to turn the equipment over to me, because he knew the equipment was there before inventory time. Instead, the count was a different amount, different items, or sometimes a series of items were missing for a period. Unable to transfer the equipment over to me in the proper manner and fashion according to regulation rules, I assured him on his departure that, although he was still responsible for all the unaccounted items and equipment, I would do everything in my power to account for the equipment so that he wouldn't end up paying for too much. I cleared all of the motor pool equipment, swapping extra items for those that we needed.

The mess hall duties were for me to oversee enlisted personnel who ran the mess hall and did the preparation of the food. There were also Austrian civilians who worked in the mess hall. Often when I went to the back of the mess hall near the rear door, I would find children going through the garbage looking for something to eat. My commanding officer instructed me that no way should I give any food to the needy, that it would disrupt the economy. To this date, I can't see how hungry people looking through the garbage could disrupt the economy. I instructed the Non-Commissioned Officers that ran the mess hall to cleanly wrap all leftover food separately. Place the edibles in a large sanitary bag, and then place it in a sanitary bin out of reach of the normal outgoing trash and away from the raw garbage. They were to seal it properly so that it would be safe to consume. After each meal those instructions were carried out to the fullest. During my stay in Austria, even though it was a short period, I'm sure I was able to feed a lot of hungry children.

In the process of trying to inventory and turn in all the equipment that was assigned to the mess hall and the motor pool, the inventory continued to grow. I had people trying to unload equipment, people were bringing me vehicles, aircrafts, heavy earth moving equipment, telling me that it belonged to me or whoever was in charge of the motor pool and it should be on my books. My crew unloaded and inventoried all of these incoming items, as minute as plates, silverware, forks, spoons. Everything had to be counted and accounted for. Much to my dismay, I knew that they had bulldozed a large land field. As they turned in much of this equipment, I was also ordered to dump this equipment into the large land field, which was burned, plowed under and covered up. Near the end of my stay and just before I left Austria, I still had those three Chevrolet sedans. I had kept them shiny-clean, always gassed up, and always ready to go on a moment's notice. They were still in the garage. I learned that those vehicles had been used for intelligence purposes only. When asked what to do with those spotless vehicles, I was told that they never existed and to dispose of them in the proper fashion. I left them in the garage with the keys in the cars and left the keys to the garage door in the door lock. As I left Austria, I often wondered who picked up three new Chevrolets. When they closed out the occupation in Salzburg, Austria, I was reassigned to Berlin, Germany.

CHAPTER 6

ARRIVING IN BERLIN

I arrived in Berlin on July 19, 1955. I found that although it was behind the Iron Curtain, it was a beautiful highly populated city. The U.S. Army Command Headquarters was in a part of the city where there was a shopping area, restaurants, theatre and a bowling alley. It was also on the fringe of the Grunewald Forest and where the U. S. Army 6th Infantry Tank Company was stationed. This location would allow a quick escape into the cover of the forest in the event of a Russian attack, which was an ongoing fear.

The nightlife was alive with nightclubs, where females outnumbered the males. That's where the fun came in. Many of the German men had left Berlin for Western Germany, where there were more opportunities for work and higher wages. Americans moved freely about the three sections, not including the Russian Section. The U.S. military was granted special orders to move into or throughout the Russian section of Berlin, where they were needed. There was a subway system and bus service that moved through the city yet stopped before entering the Russian section. The Officers' Club was in the Headquarters area and the Bachelor Officers

Quarters (B.O.Q) were nearby. Initially, I was housed in the temporary B.O.Q, as were all new officers arriving in Berlin, but, I found myself there after all of the others had been assigned to permanent quarters. When I inquired as to the reason, I was told that I would be sharing quarters with a Lt. Gardner of Medical Company and that he was in the Western Zone of Germany training for the next few weeks. I couldn't understand why they had not assigned me to some other quarters as they had the officers that arrived with me. When I learned that Lt. Gardner was also colored, I knew why they wanted me to await his return. Since it cost extra money to live in the B.O.Q. and we had to purchase all of our meals at the Officers Club, I insisted that they change the locks on the door and let me move into the three-bedroom flat that we were to share.

When Lt. Gardner returned to Berlin from Western Germany he had been promoted to Captain. He was upset that I had taken it upon myself to have the locks changed and had moved into what he felt were his quarters. We exchanged some words and since he was now two ranks my senior, I was careful as to how I addressed him. My offer to divide each room in half, since they were taking my full housing allowance, was the thing that gained his attention and we found common ground. When I learned that there were a limited number of colored officers in Berlin, I knew that the Army was not as integrated as they claimed to be. I further learned that there was an unwritten policy of limiting the total number of colored officers to approximately twelve and that I had brought the number to that limit. In talking to the other colored officers that had been there for some time, they informed me that there were other conditions that I should be aware of. Colored officers and white officers were not assigned to the same flat, apartment or single unit. They shared the same building, but not the same units.

Everyone realized that colored officers, non-commissioned officers and enlisted personnel in the Army and civilian personnel working and living in Berlin, dated German females, but they didn't want them brought to public facilities such as the officers club, company parties or other activities. I was also informed that colored officers were assigned to leadership positions, such as platoon leaders, but not in command positions such as company commanders or anything above that rank. I was also told that no colored officer had ever had his or her request to marry a German approved, nor had they been able to stay in Berlin after requesting to marry one. Captain Gardner had placed himself in a position that he would have to adhere to policy. His was the only position available for a medical company captain and that was as Company Commander. He had requested approval to marry his German fiancé. Within a very short period of time, Captain Gardner was reassigned to a unit in Western Germany. They later married and had two children.

The Sixth Infantry Regiment, to which I was assigned, was stationed in McNair Barracks and only walking distance from the flat where I was housed. My flat had three bedrooms, a formal dining room, a living room, a full kitchen, and a bathroom. It was completely furnished with everything that I needed including dishes, cooking utensils and crystal. Here I was, a poor colored officer living alone after Captain Gardner was reassigned. No more colored officers were brought to Berlin during this time. Many of my fellow officers were white and we often partied together in my flat. They couldn't understand how I lived there alone while they were crowded in other units too small for the number of officers assigned to it. They were always going to have the Army move them into my unit, but I knew that the army wouldn't, and they never did. I would allow some of them to sleep over with their dates. I would entertain friends and had some great parties in my nice large flat.

During the Christmas holidays of 1955, I invited my childhood friend, Edwin (E. J.) Nichols to visit me in Berlin. He was a student studying in Western Germany under the GI Bill and living in not so pleasant conditions. We enjoyed the holidays in Berlin. There was good food, lots of partying, drinking and sightseeing. It was a time that we both remember to this day. I was heartbroken when they built some new one-bedroom apartment B.O.Q.'s for single officers, and I was forced to move into one.

I was assigned to the Sixth Infantry Regiment. My first duty was similar to that in Austria. I was in charge of the Motor Pool and Mess Hall. Right away, I knew I had the knowledge to perform these duties and one had to figure that the commanders had to know that I had the experience. My hometown street smarts were telling me things and I acted accordingly. The majority of non-commissioned officers were driving Mercedes – the most expensive automobiles in the city. At the same time, I couldn't help but notice that our inventory was off by a great margin, and there were shortages where there shouldn't be any. Simple items such as sugar, coffee, tea and eggs were items that were hard to come by in the field.

I was responsible now, which meant that I would have to be accountable for not only some items, but also all items. I called for a meeting with all the enlisted personnel and asked for a complete inventory of what I would know when, where and how. I was met with some opposition. They tried to explain to me that they had more time in the military than I had lived, which was true in many respects, since I was only twenty. Nevertheless, I was the one in charge and I was the one who would be responsible and accountable for all items in the inventory. Once I took control of the storage room, in a brief period, the mess hall wasn't short of anything else for any reason again. Also, some of the non-commissioned officers started driving smaller automobiles.

The mess hall that I oversaw fed a number of companies. It was a consolidated mess hall and located in the building where the regional headquarters were housed. One of my regular customers who enjoyed his coffee each morning was the Commanding Officer, Colonel Walker. After talking with him on several topics and occasions over a period of time, we developed a respectful relationship. After some three months, I made the Colonel a wager. He thought it was humorous, amusing in a positive way. I bet that I could change my mess hall into one that could stand up next to a five-star restaurant on the army's inspections. He maintained the humor since he had seen none of the other mess halls ever receive such a rating, and he was fairly confident it couldn't be done. In exchange for my success, I told him I would like to be transferred from this job and to company 'D' which was a heavy weapons company. My logic in this move was that 'D-company' had vehicles; they didn't walk in training or in combat situations. The Colonel agreed to the wager and several months later, when inspection time arrived, my mess hall was found to be at the top of the rating, and I received the five-star type of rating. February 21, 1956, I was assigned to the First Battalion Company 'D' Heavy Weapons Leader 105mm.-Recoilless Rifle Platoon. The Colonel had honored the wager and me with the transfer.

In Fort Benning, Georgia, during my time with O.C.S., I had trained for this type of military position and the recoilless rifle 106 millimeter, which was more accurate and deadlier than the 105mm. The 106-millimeter was the upgraded version with higher-tech-equipment.

I was also impressed with the Company Commander, and the discipline that he had established within his company. I don't recall the Captain's name, but I had observed them in parades and other activities and was indeed impressed with their performances. Once

I was assigned to the unit, much to my dismay, I discovered that his method for obtaining discipline was to have his N.C.O.'s take enlisted people aside and physically assault them. In addition, he would have people taken outside and put into tents away from the barracks during unbearable weather, if they didn't perform or act according to his level. Since the units were in Berlin where there was limited space, and heavily populated, units were taken to the western zone for maneuvers. I had my unit in Hoeffel, Western Germany, a tactical training area, for maneuvers after we received six new 106-millimeter recoilless rifles.

The weapon was considered extremely lethal. They were anti-tank weapons. Their range was 4.78 miles. In order for me to actually fire the weapon, I had to submit a detailed plan of action for discharging such a deadly weapon to the authorities in Hoeffel for their approval. Upon approval of the range-plan, I took my unit out to field test the weapon. The 106-millimeter recoilless rifle had a fifty-caliber spotter-rifle on top of the main gun, and the main gun was mounted on the back of a Jeep, which made them extremely mobile and deadly.

I set up my unit, which consisted of six guns in three positions, with two guns each. Then I made radio contact with my section leader to inform him that we were prepared to fire. For whatever reason, I cannot explain at this time, we were firing overhead, with troops in between the impact point and us. I set up a gun personally and fired a spotter-rifle at a target down range well beyond any troops that were between the impact area and us. When the fifty-caliber spotter rifle made impact, it gave off a large puff of white sulfate smoke; I then contacted each section leader to confirm that they had indeed observed the shot. I then fired the main weapon, the 106-millimeter recoilless rifle. This made a large impact explosion. I had them verify that they had observed the procedures. In order to assure that there were no accidents, I fired to the right and left limit of the range. The maximum and minimum range was fired to identify the area where firing could take place. Once the live fire exercise started, I observed live rounds being fired down on the troops in the area below minimum range. My immediate thought was that I would be court-marshaled and sent to the military prison in Leavenworth, Kansas, for the killing of friendly troops. These rounds were dropped on our troops. I called for a cease-fire and proceeded into the area that was hit to see if there were any casualties. Thank God there were no casualties and needless to say, that was the last time we fired those weapons under those conditions in that area.

When my unit returned to Berlin following the field exercise, I requested and received a transfer out of Company 'D'. On July 10, 1956, I was assigned to First Battalion 'B' Company as a rifle platoon leader. Lieutenant William Campbell was a rifle platoon leader in Company 'B,' and was more than happy to change with me, so he transferred from Company 'B' to Company 'D'. On August 28, 1956, I coached a pistol team for the U.S. Army to victory in an allied weapons competition consisting of soldiers from America, Britain, and France. My experience had allowed me to become an expert marksman with the .45-caliber pistol. We spent weeks in training with people who were on special assignment with their only responsibility being to train and assure that there would be a victory at the competition between the three nations. My team functioned superbly, and we won the entire competition on weapons gunnery. For the success of my pistol team, I received a commendation from the Commanding Officer Colonial Glen D. Walker on September 12, 1956.

CHAPTER 7

PROMOTED TO
FIRST LIEUTENANT

On September 22, I was promoted to the rank of First Lieutenant. I exchanged my gold bars for silver. The biggest difference between a Second Lt. and a First Lt. was the increase in pay and no longer being in the lowest rank of commissioned officers. Being the rank of First or Second Lieutenant requires extra duties. Those extra duties could be as a payroll officer, training officer, testing officer, mess hall officer, motor pool officer or sometimes a legal counsel for the military court and board.

The board determined military action against the enlisted personnel that had discipline matters or problems. Filling the duties of a legal officer, I also served as defense counselor for the enlisted personnel. Those enlisted personnel who were charged with violating the Code of Military Justice, in summary, court-martial action. I found practicing the law to be exciting, encouraging and worthwhile. I used my imagination, studied the code of military justice and determined that there were loopholes that could be used in the defense of military personnel that were hardly ever used. As a matter of fact, I was told and reminded, that when other officers sent people to trial, as Defense Counselor, I was not expected to exercise too much effort on their behalf. I was expected to allow a conviction. My response was just the contrary. I told them if they assigned me as a Defense Counselor, then that assignment came first, and that I would consider that an obligation, and I would defend the enlisted personnel to the best of my ability.

My success in defending the enlisted was not met with great joy by superior or fellow officers. At one point I had been involved in eight cases and obtained eight acquittals. My reaction was that the United States Military's prosecuting attorney had the same responsibility to prove his case against my client as I had to defend the enlisted, my clients. My personal policy was that if I were to obtain an acquittal for a soldier, then I would never defend him ever again. In most cases the enlisted was either guilty as charged or charged with a greater crime in the beginning. At the end of any acquittal, I would spend time with the enlisted about never repeating an offense again. I was part counselor, and I didn't want them to ever again enlist my help as a defense counselor. Two cases come to mind. The first case concerned a soldier who had gone off base and had returned intoxicated with the aid of his friends. He was placed on the restroom floor, and the next morning he was unavailable for roll call and inspection. He was charged with failure to stand inspection along with other charges. In my cross examination of the Commanding Officer, I asked, "For the record, what instructions did you give to the guard that was placed over the intoxicated soldier?" His response was, "The guard was there to make sure that the enlisted soldier wouldn't leave." My next question was: "Did the soldier ever leave or not?" His answer was a "Definitely not, because the guard was there." I asked, "Did you instruct the guard to prepare the soldier for duty?" and he said "No! The soldier was too intoxicated." My position to the court was that the drunken soldier remained on the floor of the bathroom under guard of an armed soldier and performed the duty that he was assigned, and he never removed himself from that position. I asked for and received a summary judgment and an acquittal.

In the matter of the second case, a soldier was married to a German National who was pregnant at the time. He was on guard duty at the headquarters, and she was at home alone. They were out of contact with each other. He was very concerned, not knowing her condition. What he did know was that her delivery time was near. He wouldn't know if she had delivered or not, or if she had an accident. The worried soldier on guard duty wasn't able to have anyone relay her conditions to him or send her a message. This led him to abandon his post at the guardhouse and go check on her. When they came looking for him, he was not there. He was charged with abandoning guard duty and desertion. He was scheduled to return to United States within weeks and was upset that he would be placed in confinement and his wife would be alone with the newborn baby. Through a series of questions, I established that the guardhouse had numerous locations. Systematically I walked the witness through the search of the facility. They had established that they had searched each room but admitted they hadn't searched every room at the same time. I convinced the court that they hadn't proved that he was absent from the guardhouse. They were unable to testify that he wasn't in one of the rooms at a different time or another while they were looking for him in another at the same time. I was able to win an acquittal for him, and he and his wife and baby were able to return to the United States.

While I was assigned to the First Battalion Company 'B' as a platoon leader, there was an opening for an instructor and a training officer at Berlin Command NCO Academy. I felt that I had special skills as an instructor and indicated plans to apply for the position. I was informed that there had never been a colored instructor at the NCO (Non-Commissioned Officer) Academy and the chances of me being accepted were little to none. However, I prepared an oral presentation and was told that they were impressed by the presentation. Nevertheless, they had a better candidate. Within a matter of a couple of weeks of the rejection of my presentation, the officer from my battalion who had been appointed the position had a death in the family and had to return to the United States.

October 10, 1956, I was assigned to special duty as an Instructor and Training Officer at the Berlin Command NCO Academy. First Lieutenant Malone was our Commandant. There were two training staff officers, a Lt. Lopez and I. Six non-commissioned officers were hand-picked from the 6th Infantry Regiment because they were superior infantrymen. A normal day started at about 5:30am. After reveille, the unit would take to the road for a twenty-eight-minute run that was gradually lengthened to build stamina. From 7:30 a.m. until 9:00 a.m., there were instructions in the basic infantry weaponry and two-hour drills in hand-to-hand combat. After lunch, the students entered classroom for basic infantry instructions. I taught many classes at the NCO Academy including leadership, infantry tactics, survival training, and my specialty, weapons. As a six-week course continued, we would take members of the unit over to the Andrew Barracks swimming pool, an Olympic-size swimming pool. There, we would practice and perform abandoned ship techniques and river crossing, using ponchos and two M-1 rifles to build rafts.

While I was at the NCO academy, I developed some training aids of my own. One included a dummy that had a speaker in it. I would use the dummy attached to a tape recorder, which I used to make the dummy talk. Another tactic of mine was in teaching weapons, I would give someone in the room a firing pin that had been removed from an M-1 rifle. The firing pin had been marked with a type of colored ink. I would show them a fully assembled rifle, then turn off all the lights in the room. I would have them bring me the firing pin. In the dark I was able to disassemble, change the firing pin, reassemble the M1 rifle and fire off a couple of blanks as the soldier returned to his seat. This showed the importance of weapons knowledge to a soldier and his relationship with his M-1. On the battlefield, a soldier must know his rifle well enough to be able to change, break down, and reassemble in total darkness and make the shot. I taught survival training in such an intense way that following one presentation I was approached by a high-ranking visiting officer, who commented, "Your experience in such situations has been invaluable in your teaching." Fact was, someone who wouldn't even eat a lima bean was giving instructions on eating tree meat from under the bark and deciding which bugs and insects could be used for dinner. This was the experience from what I was teaching.

Another important part of the training process was a two-week field exercise, which we ran in the Grunewald Forest. In order to make it more realistic, I prevailed upon a friend of mine who was a disc jockey at the America Army radio station. I had him make a recorded message for me. As planned, I interrupted his radio program with the recorded announcement that the Russians had crossed over into our sector and had attacked our units. He continued saying that all personnel should report to their stations and assume battle gear and positions. I would use this tape in the Academy Mess Hall on the day that the exercise was to begin. I created a life-like situation without revealing to the NCO Academy students that this was indeed the start of the exercise. They were geared up, loaded into military trucks and transported to the forest, believing all the time that this was the real thing. The exercise was more effective at the start, with them being advised later that afternoon, it was a training exercise.

Berlin was the site and location for international visitors and on one such occasion the U.S. Commanding General with some foreign visitors was there, and we began the exercise by playing the tape. The look on the faces of the visitors was as dramatic as the expression on the faces of our cadets, although they had been previously warned that the tape was in fact fictional and was used for training purposes only. Following the beginning of that exercise, the General suggested to me that in no uncertain terms that the tape was to be destroyed for fear that it might fall into the wrong hands, played at the wrong time or wrong place and cause chaos. I never used the tape again.

During the time I was assigned to the NCO Academy, I met my wife-to-be in a club in Berlin. Vera Schwartz was a single person close to the same age as I, who like me, had never been married. Unlike many German females that I dated, Vera took me home and introduced me to her family. In many incidents, German ladies would arrange to meet soldiers somewhere in a public place, such as a restaurant, club or maybe the soldier's place. I only recall one other incident when I was dating a German girl that I was invited to her home. Vera and I started with a causal relationship where we found ourselves spending a great deal of time together. I also found both of her parents, aunts, uncles, cousins, and even her grandmother, who would visit from time to time, to be friendly and welcoming to me.

The Schwartzes were German Jews who had amassed sums of money before the war. However, they had lost most of their holdings, due to persecution by the Nazis. At the time, my use of the German language was limited; nevertheless, I could hold a reasonable conversation with her parents, grandmother and other relatives. I spent a lot of time on the weekends with the family; during the holiday season, spending time with them was always pleasant. Vera was an attractive young lady who was currently modeling, while she was still living at home with her parents in a relativity small apartment in the Schoenberg district of Berlin. As our dating became more intense, I took Vera with me to the Officer's Club, disregarding the warnings that I received about bringing German females to social events. I felt that I was a member of the Officer's Club, and my guest should be as welcome there as I was. On the first occasion that I took Vera to the club, two white officers approached me as I was going to the restroom. They told me that they personally weren't offended; however, they were carrying the message for some other officers who were offended that I had brought a white female to the Officers' Club. I asked who the other officers were and suggested that they go get them and have them tell me themselves. They said they couldn't do that, but they felt that in the effort to prevent any incidents that they would take it upon themselves to relay the information to me. My response was "I am a member, a dues paying member of the US Army Berlin Officers' Club. I will bring any guest that I choose to the Officers' Club. If any member is offended by the presence of my guest, I suggest that they stay at home because I have no intention of quitting to please someone else. I also suggested that they not carry that kind of message to me anymore and to tell whoever sent the message (even though

I believed that the message came directly from them) that they were not to send me any more messages. Vera and I visited the Officers' Club on many occasions following that incident. There were never any other situations involving Vera and me after that. As a matter of fact, after I had taken it upon myself to break this rule, other colored officers felt safe bringing their white dates to the club and did so comfortably.

Vera and I became engaged in December of 1956 and I filled out the necessary forms requesting approval of marriage. I knew that this was another one of those unwritten rules that would get me transferred out of Berlin. My attitude was that if they chose to do so, I could establish myself in a different location, wherever it might be. I continued with my duties at the Berlin Command NCO Academy until 1957. My tour of overseas duty was scheduled to end in February of 1957, and I was offered an extension. However, I chose not to accept that offer, although it was offered several times. Those offering included my immediate supervisor, higher command, and people including Commanding General of Berlin who were the ultimate persons responsible for the NCO Academy.

By January 15, 1957, I hadn't received any information concerning my request or approval to get married. Instead, I received orders to rotate to the United States. I still was attempting to marry Vera at that time and decided to take a different approach. I contacted a friend of mine who was a warrant officer in the Headquarters and asked him if he had seen my request for marriage. He said that it had not been approved and had not been returned. He didn't know the status of it. During the same conversation, he asked me if I would consider an extension of overseas service. I told him that I didn't want to extend, but I was hoping they would approve my marriage before my rotation. In a quiet manner, he suggested that I put in for an extension of service.

It was extremely unusual for the Army to change position or even accept a change of position such as mine. My rotation was to become effective February 15, 1957. On or about January 17, again by the request of my friend, the warrant officer, I agreed and allowed him to prepare the extension request documents. I signed them, still not believing that they would extend my service at that late period. The warrant officer assured me that he had reason to believe that they would do it if I would sign. Within a week, I received an extension of service and my orders for rotation to the United States were canceled, committing me to at least one additional year in Berlin. Within days, I received the marriage approval, properly signed by the commander, authorizing me to get married. Vera Schwarz and I were married on February 2, 1957. It was a memorable day – one that I'll never forget.

We were married in three separate ceremonies on the same day. In order for the marriage to be legal, we were first married in the German Court. Afterwards, we were married in the German church, and a third ceremony was conducted on the United States Army Post at McNair Barracks in the Army Chapel. I had been a regular attendee at the Protestant Services and Chapel prior to the marriage, and regularly had conversations with the chaplain. When I approached him concerning my approval to get married, he said that his religion would not permit him, nor would he perform an interracial marriage. I confronted the military authority in Berlin about his position. At that point, I was very familiar with the commanding general, as well as the Commanding Colonel of the 6th Infantry Division. They assured me that if I would tell them the date, time and place that I desired to get married, they would make sure that there was a military chaplain there to perform the service. The army flew in an army chaplain from Frankfurt, Germany, to perform the service. My recollection is that he was the Chief Chaplain in Europe at that time. He performed the service and for the third time, Vera and I were pronounced "man and wife".

At the time preceding our marriage, I was in a new B.O.Q. (Bachelors' Officers Quarters) that had been built. The facilities were one-bedroom apartments, new, very modern and efficient. But once I had made the decision to get married, it was required that I release the bachelor's quarters. All officers and military personnel had been informed if they had dependents, and either were not above the rank of captain, not approved to bring dependents to Berlin, or were not married in Berlin would not be provided with family quarters.

After Vera and I were married, we moved in with an aunt of hers by the name of Aunt Margaret. Aunt Margaret wasn't a blood relative, but more like a 'godmother' and a very close friend of Vera's mother. She lived in the vicinity of Vera's parents in a section of Berlin called Schoenberg. The hours that I worked at the Academy were long, and traveling to and from was difficult. One morning, three weeks after I was married, the Commanding General from Berlin Headquarters was visiting the NCO Academy, which was a regular activity of his. He took the time to congratulate me on my marriage and inquired as to how things were going. I explained to him that all with the Academy was going well, but that being newly married, spending so much time with my duties at the Academy and the difficulties and traveling from the apartment in Schoenberg and the Academy in Zehlendorf was causing a hardship. He asked if I was familiar with the major who was in charge of administration of housing. He and I had served together in Austria. The general told me when I got a break, I should pay him a visit.

When I had an opportunity – which I made as soon as possible – I went to visit the major and I said to him, "The General suggested that I come and visit you, does that mean that I'm going to get quarters?" The Major smiled, pointed to a map on the wall and a board that contained keys to various apartments and said, "Those that are marked in red are vacated, make your selection and tell me which one you want." To my knowledge there were no first lieutenants in the family quarters, which were two or three-story buildings. Assignment to the building was according to rank, with junior-captains on the second and third floor, seniors-captains on the first floor. I selected a first-floor corner apartment that was larger than some of the rest and Vera and I moved in. The apartment was rather new, completely furnished, and made an excellent home for a couple that were newlyweds. The people in the building were friendly, but I'm sure they were concerned as to how I had obtained a first-floor apartment, especially in such a short notice. They were carrying their laundry and groceries up the steps because there was no elevator in the building.

There was a Captain Davis and his wife who lived on the second floor. Captain Davis and I were associates at one time when we were assigned to the same First Battalion. Captain Davis and his wife were from the South and his wife, a Southern belle, wasn't particularly happy that a colored officer and a German female lived in the building, and the fact that they occupied the first-floor corner apartment. I knew that she spent time visiting with other wives in the building, making insulting and derogatory statements about us, but I didn't let it affect our relationship. On occasions, we attended the same social affairs together, and we would see her periodically in the building. On one such occasion we attended a party at the home of the commanding colonel of the battalion, Colonel Clarey. Captain Davis's wife overindulged and became intoxicated to the point that someone suggested that Captain Davis take her home.

Since we had gone to the party in the same vehicle and I was driving when we first returned home, I let the women off at the entrances of the apartment building, I then asked my wife, Vera, to go in and fix the captain's wife a drink. Since Vera didn't drink and knew very little about portions to mix a drink, she would pour as much as half the glass and that's what she did when she fixed the captain's wife her drink. By the time the captain and I went to park the car and enter my apartment, the captain's wife was a happy drunk. The captain's wife, now a happy drunk, decided to get comfortable, so she flipped up her formal wear and pulled off her nylons and shoes exposing her underclothes. She then looked at me and said, "Hey sugar, you want to dance?"

I danced with the Captain's wife and she held me close and was extremely affectionate. Shortly after that, Mrs. Davis finished her drink and passed out, putting her husband in an apologizing circumstance, an embarrassing moment for him. I assured him that it wasn't a big thing and I would assist him in taking her home upstairs and help put her to bed. With him holding her head and me holding her legs and feet we hauled Mrs. Davis into the apartment and put her to bed. After allowing Captain Davis to apologize again for his wife's behavior, I reassured him that it wasn't a big thing, I left smiling, laughing all the way out, and loudly, after turning up the Hi-Fi stereo in the apartment so no one could hear me. Nobody saw Mrs. Davis for a couple of weeks. She went out the back door or ducked around to keep from making eye contact out of embarrassment.

Near the end of April of 1957, Lt. Colonel Thomas Clarey, the new Commander of the First Battalion 6th Inf. Regiment paid me a visit at the NCO Academy. He was my commanding officer, although I was on special duty assignment to the NCO Academy and not reporting to him at that time. He informed me that he had reviewed my record, observed me instructing at the Academy and desired that I return to his unit, if he could obtain a release from the commanding general. He asked me if I would be agreeable to such an arrangement, to which I replied positively, because I realized that he was, in fact, my commander. After several days, Colonel Clarey contacted me; he obtained my release upon sending an accurate replacement. He also wished that I would join him as a member of his staff. Since battalion staff officers were generally captains or majors and because we were receiving large numbers of officers who were returning from Korea, I was surprised that he had offered me the position.

Many of the officers who were assigned to the First Battalion were higher in rank and there were captains and some majors who were returning at that time. At the same time that the offer was made, I was a First Lieutenant with no more than eight months in grade. I inquired as to which staff position he was offering me. He replied, "Your choice. I know that you can do any one of them." The battalion staff included an S-1, a battalion adjutant, an administrator for the commander, and one who issues orders and acts in his behalf; the S-2, who is the intelligence officer. The S-3 is an operations officer. In addition, is the S-4, the logistic officer. There was also an executive officer that was generally a Major. That job was not offered to me. I chose the job of S-1 adjutant because I thought it would give me the most flexibility, and the adjutant was assigned a jeep and driver in conjunction with his duties.

On May 1st I was assigned back to the First Battalion Headquarters as a Battalion Adjutant. I understand, before my return, directly after the announcement of my return as the S-1 Adjutant that there was a loud uproar. This uproar was brought under control when the Colonel, stated that, it was his command. It was his decision to make, and he had made his decision. Anyone who failed to comply and or failed to cooperate with any orders from the S-1 could and would be court-marshaled.

At twenty-two years old and a First Lieutenant with less than eight-months of seniority, I believe that I may have been the youngest black and lowest ranking Battalion Adjutant in the United States Army in an integrated unit in 1957. I functioned in the capacity of S-1 until September 1957 without incident. During my tenure as Battalion S-1, the whole unit of the First Battalion packed its entire gear, all of its equipment and manpower and traveled to the western zone of Germany for maneuvers and field efficiencies test that were administered by the United States Department of Army and the Pentagon. That test involved a field exercise and mock warfare operation. Included in my duties were the advanced movements of the units to various locations, the establishment of communications, the setting up of the headquarters, and the issuing of various orders in connection with movements. We completed that exercise, during which time each staff member was graded. My grade was an eighty-eight-point-nine, (88.9). The grade of each of the four staff members counted for 15% percent, and the grade of the commanders counted for 25% percent, which meant that the performance of each of the four companies combined and their commanders counted for only 15% percent. In my recollection, all four companies failed the test, but the Battalion score was approximately 86% percent.

Following the test, the unit returned to Berlin and I functioned in the capacity of S-1 within our barracks. I became a very good friend of the Colonel and his wife, who became fond of Vera and took her in almost as if she were their daughter. The wives spent much of their leisure time together, and we all attended social affairs at their home. At this point, I had managed to obtain and be certified with others with the distinction of Military Occupational Specialty (MOS). This was the result of my full knowledge as a mess officer, motor officer, rifle platoon leader, anti-tank platoon leader, an instructor, and a battalion adjutant. In addition, I had obtained certification in chemical, biological, radiology warfare, and military training in safety, with expertise in all weapons the military used at that time.

In September of 1957, the doctor informed us that Vera was pregnant. On September 15, 1957, I made a formal request of the military that they allow me to rotate back to the United States early to prevent my wife having to travel in her late stages of her pregnancy. We were also told that the date of birth was such that we could probably end up remaining in Berlin with the baby for some time beyond the rotation date, if we didn't rotate in the early stages. That request was denied. We remained in Berlin for the full duration of my extension.

In early November, while Vera was still able to travel, we took a trip around Europe to view some other parts to Europe. I took a fourteen-day leave, and we obtained orders from the military for both of us to travel to the western portion of Germany. There was a restriction preventing Vera's travel by U.S. Army automobile through the Russians sector. I arranged to meet her at the Russian checkpoint on the western side. Traveling by automobile to Dusseldorf where she had lived for a short period and worked as a young adult, we visited with friends, shopped, and enjoyed life as tourists. We went on to Paris, France, visited Luxemburg and Belgium. We went into Holland and visited Switzerland, returning to Western Germany before our trip back through the Russian sector. Before we arrived at the checkpoint, I arranged with a German family, that we had met, to have Vera transported. Vera left ahead of me and I followed driving a used, older model Plymouth. One-fourth of the way there I had car problems and the vehicle overheated.

There was concern for officer personnel traveling through the Russian sector that they would disappear and be missing for a long period while the Russians held them without the military knowing where they were. Sitting out on the road in a thunderstorm's downpour, I was concerned that Russian military personnel or any other Russian authorities would come by and take me into custody. I managed to collect enough rainwater off of the ground by using towels and other things to fill the radiator to get the vehicle started. While sitting there, a large double tracker-trailer vehicle pulled-up in front of me seeing that I was in trouble. The German driver that was in front of me was now concerned because I was a United States Military officer. He insisted that I not be left out there to an awful fate. He insisted that he would somehow tow my vehicle. But we didn't have any towing equipment other than a couple of short chains that were hanging from the rear of his trailer. In the pouring rain, we managed to link them together.

My obvious thoughts were that the German driver who had come to my aid would drive at an appropriate speed, as he was indeed towing another vehicle. The weather conditions were a major factor. I couldn't have been more wrong! I watched as the speedometer indicated the thirty, forty, -fifty, sixty, seventy, eighty, ninety miles per hour. The old Plymouth was unsteady, unstable, my windshield wipers weren't working, and my horn wasn't working as the speed reached one hundred miles per hour. The vehicle was swaying from left to right with only a short-linked chain that was attached from the rear of his trailer to the front of mine. I was being dragged and thrown around like it was a toy. After about forty or fifty miles, the driver of the truck pulled into a rest stop. By then I was a basket case, thinking that I was going to die at any minute. Once I was convinced that the vehicle had come to a safe stop, I jumped out for fear that the driver would seemly pull through the rest stop and keep on going. I informed the driver that I would rather take my chance out in the rain with the Russians instead of taking a chance of the chain braking while I was in the car dangling dangerously.

We removed the chains and cooled the engine. I was able to drive back into Berlin. I arrived at the eastern military checkpoint just as they were preparing to dispatch a search party for me. When you traveled through the Russian sector by automobile or by convoy, they clock you 'out' at the western section, and in at the eastern checkpoint based on the approximate travel time.   If personnel were gone too long, they suspected that they had fallen prey to Russian interceptors and would send military search parties to learn of their disposition. I arrived home to an excited and concerned Vera, who had arrived hours earlier with the family. She was even more concerned when I relayed my ordeal and lived to tell the tale.

In order not to have to wait until after the child was born, Colonel Thomas Clary and his wife, who were rotating in early January, agreed to take Vera back to the United States. Pennsylvania was their hometown and Vera could stay with them until my rotation date came up, sometime later in the month. I completed my tour of duty with Company 'C' First Battalion, closed out our apartment and left Germany, January 23, 1958, aboard the SS United States. The Army afforded me first-class passage and I enjoyed this trip, except that I was traveling alone without my new wife. I was sharing a cabin with two other officers, both white. We had a wonderful trip. One was a chaplain, who enjoyed the spirits as much as the other officer and I. The food was excellent, the excitement was fun, and the trip was luxurious. I used the occasion to visit the spa, something that I had never done before and something that I have not done since.

I arrived in New York and made contact with Vera at the Clarey's home. They brought her to New York City and that's where we had our reunion. We spent two days in New York City in a hotel and we did some sightseeing. Some of the glances that we received in New York City reminded me that this was not Germany, and our marriage wouldn't be widely accepted as it had been in Berlin. The military, her family, friends and I had arranged to bring a vehicle back to the States from Germany. After picking it up, we proceeded to my parent's home in Detroit, Michigan, via New York, Pennsylvania and an Ohio toll-road. We arrived in Detroit safely, even though the weather had been very bad. Icy roads were all along the way, and we experienced some near misses.

Upon arrival in Detroit, I had a chance to introduce my new bride, and their new relative for the first time. Although my family was cordial, it was a new experience for them; this being the first time someone had brought a person of another race into the family. I now realize how such a change affects so many members of a family. I had not anticipated it then. Vera spoke English but with an accent; however, she was able to converse with members of the family and our friends relatively easy.

I was on leave before reporting to Fort Riley, Kansas on March 3, 1958. I left Vera in Detroit with my parents who were living in a very large family home on the west side of Detroit at that time. All of the other siblings had left home by then and my parents were alone in the house that had at least six bedrooms. Vera, of course, wanted to be with me, but it was impossible for her to travel. Denise Renee was born on March 28, 1958, in Detroit, Michigan. I was still in the Army, assigned to Fort Riley and after having a twenty-day leave. I couldn't be home in Detroit at the time of her birth, but shortly afterwards Vera and Denise came to Fort Riley.

I still hadn't received any family quarters nor was I assigned to a unit. Vera and Denise had to return to Detroit. My arrival at Fort Riley wasn't warmly received. I was still a Junior-First Lieutenant at the time, but my military record showed a great deal of experience. By the time I arrived there, I had several Military Occupation Specialists, yet they were not ready to assign me. In different temporary capacities, I worked with personnel, training men in weapons specializing in pistol-marksmanship. I also performed other administrative tasks for a while as they claimed they could not assign me to a unit because the military had gone to a new concept of organization, and the 6th Infantry Regiment from where I had been assigned was what they called a conventional infantry regiment.

On April 3rd I received orders that I was being assigned to temporary duty assignment for 164 days at Camp McCoy, Wisconsin, with the report date of April 12, 1958. The assignment was an MOS -5000, which was the Post Special Services Officer. I did not have this MOS, nor had I ever acted in that capacity. The services called for a higher-ranking officer with reasonable experiences that I did not have. When I arrived at Camp McCoy and reported in, the commander who read my personnel file realized that I had been improperly assigned. He said that he wouldn't place me in the position because I lacked the experience, and that the assignment would only cause me trouble. He also said that should have been obvious to those that assigned me. He reassigned me back to Fort Riley, Kansas. When I returned to Fort Riley, Kansas, I reminded them that I was married and that I was a new father and I desired to have my family with me. They continued to vacillate about assigning me to another temporary assignment and told me that they were looking for another assignment for me. That temporary assignment, although they didn't tell me, would have taken me from my home base where I could not request quarters.

By this time, I realized that my military record and the fact that I was interracially married were contributing to their inability to find an assignment for me to meet my military obligations. I requested that I be released from the United States Army active duty. I was released from active duty on May 18, 1958, and returned to my family in Detroit, Michigan. Although the military encouraged that I get involved in some type of active reserved unit, I did not do so, which was a wise decision. If I had, I would have been called up for service in Vietnam.

PART THREE
OUT OF THE MILITARY

CHAPTER 8

RETURNING TO CIVILIAN LIFE

May 19, 1958, after having been released from active duty in the United States Army, I returned to my family in Detroit. Vera and I set up house in the near Westside of Detroit in a two-story flat, occupying the second floor. We had purchased new furniture while we were in Berlin and had it shipped to the United States. We were able to put this new furniture in our newly decorated house, and we felt comfortable. Even though the neighborhood was interracial, there were more coloreds than whites within our immediate area. We made friends and met our neighbors. We were reasonably happy at that time, but I did not realize that, when I left the service, the country was in the throes of a recession, and that there was extremely limited work in the Detroit area. My experiences in the military were of little or no use in civilian life. There were no jobs for military commanders or weapons specialists. I looked for work and took whatever I could find at that time. My experiences in repair came in handy, as I found myself doing maintenance work, which included carpentry, plumbing, electrical, and other repairs. I believed as a returning vet, an ex-military officer, I would be able to find work in the administration field where I could use my skills. We had purchased a new Ford Fairland 500 in 1958 when we first returned to Detroit, using my father's discount as a representative of the UAW (United Auto Workers). The payment on the car was not great, but with me being unable to find any work, our savings started to become depleted quickly. The expenses of the new baby, Denise, and a new marriage began to add up quickly.

Vera was able to find work in Detroit and went to work in a downtown store. In addition, she also looked for work as a model, since that had been her experience in Berlin. Being new to the country and seeing the availability of goods and services that were available were beyond Vera's comprehension. She soon became anxious to have the many finer things in life and have them immediately. I tried to convince her that we could not afford many of these things, but they would come in due time if she would wait for a while. Unfortunately, Vera didn't need my approval to open charge accounts and did so at many of Detroit's downtown stores near where she worked. I took a job in the evening, acting as a disc jockey at a local club. I had purchased a good collection of jazz albums as a bachelor in Berlin, and I had purchased a state-of-the-art high-fidelity unit. I was able to convince the lounge owner that I could increase his business by acting as disc jockey several nights a week. Although this brought revenue into the house, it also created problems. The fact that I worked evenings and into the closing hours of the bar, which was one to two in the morning, put a strain on us.

I asked my father if he could assist me by helping me obtain employment. Since he was an international representative of the UAW, and had contact with various auto plants, he was able to find me a job, but it was in a foundry in Detroit. A foundry is a plant where large castings are made. In a foundry, they build molds out of sand, some of them are 10 x 12 x 6 feet high. These molds are then filled with molten iron that's heated in the plant furnace, called cupolas. The cupolas in this foundry were loaded by dumping from a wheelbarrow, scrap steel, iron, coke, and other chemicals into a conveyer with a huge bucket, which lifted them to the roof of the cupolas, which deposit it down into the fire. The operator of the cupolas, which I became, is then the receiver of burning ash and cinders that land in your gloves, on your neck and back. The fire burns at a temperature hot enough to melt steel and iron. The iron is then poured off the cupolas into ladles and transported by crane to the areas of the molds. When the iron is poured into the molds, it creates dirt, dust, soot, fumes, and smoke. During the months that I worked in the foundry, I determined that if you spend any time in a foundry you would get a free pass from going to hell, because you had already been there.

On December 2, 1959, Vera and I were blessed with a second daughter, Monique Yvette Bowman. She was a beautiful healthy baby and we celebrated the blessing of her birth. Around this time,

I had applied for a position with the United States Postal Service and was excited when I received the news that I had passed the test for the position of postal clerk and was eligible for employment. I resigned my job at the foundry, thinking that I was going to better myself. Shortly after accepting the position of clerk at the post office, they assigned me as a mail-handler. I spent most of my days dragging large bags of mail around on docks, putting them on trucks and conveyers. When I did sort mail, it was packages and on an extremely limited basis. The post office said that since I was classified as a temporary postal clerk, it was a necessary requirement that I learn a scheme, all of the street locations, zip codes, and sort mail to the extent where I met the requirement of a clerk. There were no indications that they intended to use me in that capacity, and I continued to work on the dock indoors and out for long hours. As a temporary clerk (mail-handler), I was required to report to work whenever I was told, and to perform whatever work was assigned to me without questioning how many hours I would work, or how many days a week I would be at the job. I was told that, as a temporary employee, I had no 'rights' and they could assign me to whatever they wanted, for whatever they wanted for however many days they chose.

The atmosphere in the post office was extremely undisciplined, when applied to permanent postal personnel. I observed people coming into work intoxicated, drinking on the job, remaining intoxicated, and sleeping on the job in the open and in the restroom.

These people were not corrected or disciplined. Many times, when we were loading vehicles on the dock, they stood or sat or did nothing. I found myself constantly working long hours and being confronted by the superiors because I was temporary. If I slowed down to take a break or did anything that they thought wasn't proper, I was reprimanded while permanent employees were not.

To this date, 2009, the United States Post Office has the dubious distinction of being the only job that I quit without first having another job and where I would never work again in my life. Having quit the post office, I found myself unable to find other work, and took my tools back into the maintenance business. Although I worked long hours, I was unable to generate enough revenue to support my family in the manner in with which they had grown accustomed. In early June of 1961, I developed a business plan to open a marketing company. Vera and I incorporated Quality Service, Inc. on June 14,1961.

This was done after I had rented a storefront on the west side of Detroit. I worked hard to sub-divide it into office sections, decorated and furnished it with used furniture. The marketing concept was to bring companies in under the umbrella of Quality Service, Inc. and to do advertising and marketing, based on the concept that we endorse these companies that pledge to provide only Quality Service to the public. The concept was slow starting in that I did all of the concept materials, designed all of the forms, and did all of the paperwork myself. I engaged a lawyer who incorporated the company, and we were given a very broad license that allowed us to do many things. I developed a contract that I sold to businesses starting in the immediate neighborhood of my office in what was generally a minority neighborhood. In the beginning, the contract sold for $9 a quarter or $36 a year. As a member, you were able to display the Quality Service, Inc. decal on your door and my company would advertise through the use of newspaper, radio, and eventually television so that the public would seek out the businesses that displayed the Quality Service, Inc. seal and patronize those who had pledged themselves to provide only quality service. To encourage patronage, we provided entry forms at member locations for customers to participate in monthly drawings for prizes such as TV's, radios and watches at no cost to the member businesses. In fact, what I was selling was a concept of co-op advertising and customer service through referrals and endorsements. During this time, on July 24, 1961, the stork paid Vera and me another visit, and Frederick Jr. became our first son. My family and other friends thought I had gone crazy and told me that nobody would buy the program. Cash was at a minimum and I found myself the number one salesman, generating enough revenue to keep the doors open. I advertised for salespeople but was unable to keep a number of them because it was only on commission, and the contract was so small it took a large volume of contracts to make a living. The concept caught on and we raised the price of the contract from $9 a quarter to $10 a month, which meant then that the contract sold for $120 per year.

I found myself spending long hours in the office, attempting to hire people, working in the field making sales calls, and trying to develop new strategies that would result in more sales. My family life started to deteriorate, and Vera said she wanted me out of the house. I moved into the back of the office with limited resources at the time and found myself working and living out of the office. On one occasion, when I had a terrible toothache and insufficient funds, I went in the back of the office one evening, took a large drink of whiskey, took a pair of pliers out of my tools and extracted the tooth myself. On another occasion I was having difficulty paying the electric bill and the utilities company turned off my power. With my knowledge of maintenance, I ran a power line from my main box through the basement to the business next door, which happened to be a barbershop. I hooked into their power system but was extremely careful to only burn a small lamp in front of the business. One Saturday, I was having a sales meeting when someone said the building was too dark, and they immediately walked over and switched on a set of florescent lights attached to the ceiling, generating a need for enough power so that it blew out the power in my place and in the business next door. I quickly turned off the ceiling light and descended the stairway to the basement that we shared. I went ahead and extracted the line that I had run to the barbershop, rolled up the wiring, and hid it in the ceiling on my side of the building. I then exited the back door, came around the building, to the front door, after I had turned the barbershop lights back on. Once the barbershop was satisfied with their lights being back on, I returned to the basement, hooked up the wiring, with one light burning and I completed my sales meeting.

Early one afternoon on a Friday, I looked out the front window and observed what I thought was a bill collector coming toward my building. I had some salespeople in the building, along with an associate of mine who was helping me develop the business and who realized how strapped my finances really were. I quickly dismissed the salespeople and remained with the associate. The bill collector entered the door. I met him and suggested that I knew what he was here for. His response was "And what do you think I'm here for?" I said, "You're looking for Frederick Bowman, he probably owes you money." His reply was "Yes." My response was, "I am tired of people coming to my place of business looking for my twin. I am Fred Bowman." I further explained to him that since my brother Frederick Bowman had caused me so much difficulty having bill collectors and others mistaking us, I thought perhaps I would give him the location where he could contact Frederick. In his anxiety, he promised not to tell Frederick that I told him where he was. After vacillating for a while, I gave him the address on the Far East side where I realized it would take him an hour to travel and return. I also gave him an address where there was probably nothing, much less a home or business. He thanked me and left. My associate was astonished and said that this was the first time he had ever seen anyone deny himself. I assured him that I was not crazy, but that I was desperate, and the ends justified the means in this case.

The bill collector returned in approximately an hour and forty-five minutes, and he was furious. He approached and said "You sent me to a vacant lot. I don't even believe that you're a twin. You're probably Fredrick Bowman." I confirmed my identity. I then proceeded to dress him down by telling him that this was my place of business, and he couldn't come here and attempt to collect his bills. I explained that my success depended on salespeople who, if they thought I couldn't pay my bills wouldn't believe that I could pay them. I admonished him that people like him would put people like me out of business, and nobody would collect any money. I told him never to come back to my business again. He left a little bit confused, but following my instructions, he never returned. My associate looked at me and said, "I don't believe you just did that."

In my effort to obtain more professional salespeople, I made contact with a gentleman who had executive sales experience. He was intrigued with the concept of the program and the possibility of its success. He agreed to come in as my sales manager. In addition, he took the business plan to a group of bankers in Lansing, Michigan, and obtained some venture capital. We moved the business out of the storefront into a business complex that was more impressive. We had a reception area, telephones, and other equipment. He was able to hire other salespeople, and we raised the contract to over $400 dollars per year. As we continued to sell more of the contracts and extend beyond the minority area to other parts of Detroit into the wealthy suburbs, the Michigan Attorney General's Office became suspicious. We were summoned to the Attorney General's Office to prove that we were lawful and operating within the limits of our articles of incorporation. We had developed and were keeping proper books, reports, and following the articles of incorporation. After viewing all of the materials, the Attorney General's Office said that they were surprised the degree and extent to which our business had authority to operate.

The general concept was that we would identify and take into membership at least one type of service business in each postal zone around the metropolitan Detroit Area. We would then advertise so that patrons would look for the Quality Service Seal on business doors and windows that were pledged to provide quality service. We would also set up telephone lines where customers could call one telephone number for many types of services, i.e., plumbing, electrical, carpet cleaning, barber, hardware, automobile repair, restaurant, and others. All were pledged to provide quality service and we would refer our members to them.

In early 1962, Vera realized that I had moved the business into the new complex. She did not understand the concept of corporation and that monies were not mine to disburse. She asked me to transfer some money to her, which I couldn't because the business was still struggling. I was unable to extract any more than basic expenses that I could properly account for. At the time, my mother was babysitting the children, and Vera was paying her a small fee. One day Vera asked me to meet her at a restaurant, where she arrived with a friend of hers. She acknowledged that I had asked for and was desirous of custody of the children since our initial separation, which she refused. She presented me with a proposal that I would pay her $1,000 per child ($3,000), and she would then sign over custody to me. Although extremely angry and possessed with feelings of violence, I told her that I didn't have that type of money and further, that she could not sell me my children.

Within two weeks, I received a call from my mother, about 3:15 pm, and was told that she could no longer watch the kids, that I needed to pick them up by 5:00 p.m. By then, I had rented a small studio apartment with a Murphy bed in it. Vera had kept all of the furniture, utensils and items from the house. I had only my personal belongings. I picked up the three children, Fred being the youngest at 8 months, and brought them back to the apartment with all of their clothing, formula, and diaper bag. That evening, I fed them. I went to the store and brought a Kellogg Variety Cereal Pack and some plastic spoons. I fixed formula for the baby that evening, and the next morning fed the girls, then 3 and 2 years old, using the variety pack box as a cereal bowl. I then bathed and dressed them. I was still tired because the night before, I had tried to sleep in the bed with the three children and found that there were no sides on the bed and that one or two of the children kept falling off. I ended up kneeling on the floor beside the bed, placing them in the center of the bed and wrapped my arms around them to keep them from falling out. It had been a restless night and I had gotten very little sleep. A close friend of mine, Gamwell Simpson, (who was much more like brother than a friend) had told his sister about my plight and she had agreed to allow me to bring the children to her house, and she would watch them while I attempted to figure out what I was going to do with the business. I did not own an automobile at the time. After the children were dressed, I took them across the street to the bus stop and waited for the Linwood bus going north. I stood there with Fred, Jr., in my arms, holding the hand of Monique, who was 3 years old, and Denise who was 4 years old grabbing onto my pant leg. I had the diaper bag over my shoulder, with extra diapers and a change of clothes for the girls, the baby bag, and some formula in it. I stood there, thinking that I had no idea how I was going to keep my little family together, and wondering if perhaps my God had forsaken them and me.

As I approached the bus stop, there was a little old woman standing there about 80 years of age who watched me approach. At that time, I felt as if I were so fragile, that if anyone said something to me, touched me, or made any motion in my direction, I would probably collapse. I refused to look at the little old woman who was staring at the children and me. Unable to control myself, I made eye contact with her at which time she spoke, "Son, you sure are in the baby business." Her voice penetrated my soul, for truly I was in the baby business. That morning began one of the greatest adventures of my life and the lives of my children.

After leaving the children with Gamwell's sister, I proceeded to the office to meet with my General Sales Manager and his associates who had made the investment in the company. After discussing my plight, and the fact that I now had custody of the children, we reviewed some possible options with them making an offer. Their offer was that they would buy a sufficient amount of stock in the company, at a reasonable face value. This would allow me enough funds to place the children in some type of care facility and free me up to continue to run the company. They said that they were not knowledgeable enough about the concept and the direction of the company to run it without me. Since I had been strapped for money for such a long period, the offer appeared to be a workable one, but the thought of placing my children in someone else's care was more than I could imagine. I rejected their offer. That evening I locked the door at the office facility, leaving all monies in the bank, leaving all materials and equipment in the office, and I never returned to the business.

CHAPTER 9

JUST THE FOUR OF US!

It was the second day following the mandate from my mother that she would no longer assist in caring for the children; I had to pick them up from her home. I had a temporary solution for watching the kids, but I needed to determine how I was going to generate enough revenue to establish a home for them. Vera had kept all of the furniture and personal belongings and having lived in a studio apartment with a Murphy type pull down bed, I had not accumulated any additional furniture. My housewares consisted of a couple of small pots, a frying pan, a couple of dishes and cups and a few pieces of silverware. This is all that I needed to sustain myself in a bachelor environment.

Since I had locked the door on Quality Service Incorporated and taken no funds or items from the business, the only thing that I could do to generate money quickly was to pull out my tools and go back into the maintenance business. My tools were extremely limited and consisted of a small number of hand tools and a power saw and power drill. I was prepared to make the best of what I had. I contacted some of the people I had done work for before, produced a few flyers advertising the fact that I was a capable handyman with knowledge of electrical, carpentry, plumbing and other household and small appliance repairs and generated a reasonable amount of business.

One of the problems that I was faced with was that for all the time I was working, I had to arrange for babysitting. None of the children were old enough for school, just yet. I made contact with a friend of mine from grade school and high school, who was a very close friend of mine – more like a good brother. Gamwell Simpson was married and had two children approximately the same age as mine. His wife and his sister were very helpful in watching the children during the day, and I was able to pay someone to watch them in the evenings when I was working on projects and was away from the apartment. I also realized that I needed to work out other arrangements for the children as far as living quarters because the small studio apartment did not have space for beds, and the children needed beds of their own. The only piece of furniture I had at this time was a new High-Fidelity system that I purchased in a furniture store in Detroit, which had extended credit to me without knowledge of how deeply in debt I was, at the time. Although it was probably not a very wise investment, this item was the only enjoyment that I had and the only item that gave me any type of pleasure in the apartment, while I was separated from my family.

E.J., Edwin Nichols, a very good friend of mine, even to this day, reappeared in my life about the time I took custody of the children. He realized I needed a place to stay and came to my assistance with financial help, daily contact, support and encouragement. I located an available flat in the area where Vera and I originally lived when we returned to the United States from Europe. The flat had four bedrooms but was unfurnished. I was producing enough revenue through the maintenance business to rent the flat and E.J. and I set out to furnish it. We obtained some gifts, donations from E.J.s' family and other friends of mine and we visited thrift stores, Salvation Army stores, Goodwill stores and other places that had used furniture, utensils and housewares. We acquired enough bedding and furnishings to furnish the place and make it respectable and moved the children into the flat. The children were very helpful at that point and quite pleased to be with me. They made inquiries about their mother and her whereabouts, which I gave them the best possible positive answer I could come up with, and that was that she wasn't available and had chosen to do something else at that time.

While struggling with paying rent and utilities, as well as providing for supervision and care for the children while I was out-performing maintenance work, I found myself more and more under pressure. I felt that if I could hire a housekeeper, someone who could move into the house in one of the bedrooms and watch the kids for more than eight hours, this would allow me more time to do more work and to generate more revenue. I put out the word that I was looking for a live-in housekeeper and even ran an ad in the newspaper. At that point, I had not given much thought to the fact that I was a twenty-seven-year-old man looking for some female to move into the house and share living quarters. The year was 1961 and things weren't like they are today. Older women responded to my newspaper ad, which proved to be very difficult. Many thought I was looking for a mother for myself and would give me a long list of things that they would and would not do. That list consisted of telling me which days they would work, what they would and wouldn't do, what I could and couldn't do, what I should and shouldn't do and what the children had better do. When younger women responded to the ad and realized I was a young person, their reaction was that I was looking for a bed partner and they rejected any possible offers. I found myself paying for a babysitter in the day - in many cases -one in the afternoon, and one when I needed to be out in the evening. If I had an activity late at night, it required a different person or extended payments for overtime.

No government program would assist me, as federal aid was primarily designed for White, female widows. Vera did not contribute any money or time, very little assistance came from my family, and most people thought that a man left with children by their mother had to be an awful person. I couldn't generate money to cover all of these costs and found myself in dire poverty.

E.J. Nichols came by often to encourage me, provided me with whatever money he could spare, and sometimes brought food for the children and me. Gamwell Simpson and his family, who lived nearby, also supported me with encouragement, gave whatever financial assistance they could, and shared food with me. Gamwell was going through the same crisis as I was. Having come out of the Army about the same time, he was also unable to find gainful employment. He and I took on all sorts of projects together, including working in auto washes, bowling alleys, day labor, and in the winter, shoveling snow or whatever we could find to do to generate money. Through my continuous effort to find someone to move into the house, a seventeen-year-old young woman answered one of my ads by the name of Delphine. I explained to Delphine that I needed someone to move into the house and care for the children while I worked. We talked for a long time, and I tried to be as honest with Delphine as I could explaining to her that I knew that moving in with a young man might cause difficulty with her family and that people would possibly talk, saying that I had moved in a girlfriend and that I was having a relationship. Delphine responded that she would be honest with me and explained that she was in the early stages of pregnancy and that her boyfriend, the baby's father, was in the military. She also told me that her parents were upset with the pregnancy and that they had asked her to move out of the house. She said she needed a place to stay and that being with the children and working with them, would make her a better parent when her child arrived. I was elated, as were the children. They were happy to have a female in the house with them at all times.

Delphine proved to be more than capable of taking care of the children, and they developed a very good relationship. She kept the kids clean, fed, and well-groomed. She spent time with them, and the environment was more stable. The pressure continued since I had taken on the responsibility to pay Delphine, to feed her, and to pay the additional expenses that went with the house and the children. I found myself working longer hours and having less time with the children and none for myself. In addition, I was having difficulty obtaining sufficient work in the maintenance area to generate the type of revenue that the home needed.

By July 1962, I had determined that the maintenance business was not sufficient, nor could I provide health insurance for the children and sustain the house on the monies I was making. I had discussions with both Gamwell and E.J. about the possibility of my going to Cleveland, Ohio, to seek work. My explanation to them was that, earlier on in my life, I had lived in Cleveland and found work; and I thought that the job market in Cleveland allowed for more diversity. I thought that I would be able to find some type of work there and that it wasn't heavily dependent on the auto industry, as was Detroit. This was a very difficult decision in that I knew that I could not pick the kids up and take them to Cleveland with me while I looked for work, so I had to consider leaving the children in someone else's care if I did make the move to Cleveland. I had no difficulty making that commitment when the following happened.

Late in August, I found a truck at the flat and two men repossessing the High-Fidelity system that I had purchased during the time when I lived in the studio apartment, the only piece of furniture that I had following the separation. I could not understand how the company had located where we were living and the only ones that knew we were there were Gamwell, E.J., my family, and a few close friends, none of which I thought would be in the position, nor would they tell this company where I was. Much to my dismay, I learned later that a family member of mine, a sister, had told the company what my address was. When I asked her why she had seen fit to tell them, when no member of my family had done anything to assist the children and me or had even come by to see if we were alive, she said she thought she had an obligation to do so.

I decided to move to Cleveland. I did not discuss the move with my parents or my brothers or sisters because I felt they did not care. When I discussed the move with Gamwell and E.J., they assured me they would support me in any way possible, and if I did go, they would look after the children and make sure Delphine would have anything she needed to sustain them while I was away.

One afternoon in mid-August, with the assurance of two of my closest friends that they would keep an eye on my home and the children, I packed a small briefcase with as much clothing as I could fit in it. I had one change of clothes, two changes of underwear and socks and some personal hygiene equipment. I did not pack a larger suitcase because I didn't have any means of transportation. I walked to my friend Gamwell's house to tell him I was headed to Cleveland, Ohio. "How are you getting there?" he asked, "by bus?" I answered, "I'm walking." "How much money do you have?" he said. "Five dollars", I said. "Come with me." he commanded, and we went to the nearest grocery store. He asked for my five dollars. He took eight dollars out of his pocket. He asked the clerk for ten singles and four quarters. We left the market and stood on Linwood Ave., Gamwell stood there and counted one dollar for me and one dollar for him, one dollar for me and one dollar for him, until we had both six dollars and fifty cents. Then he said, "I am sorry this is all the money I've got, but at least you now have as much as I have."

I had driven from Detroit to Cleveland on occasion, so I knew the route well. I took one of the quarters and boarded the city bus and took it as far as the city bus would go. After exiting the bus, I walked to Telegraph Road and started walking in the direction of Cleveland. I was carrying the briefcase, which grew heavier as I continued to walk, and I kept changing hands along the road. I walked in the evening hours and occasionally put up a thumb hoping someone would give me a ride. After about three hours of walking, a truck driver stopped and gave me a ride to the Toledo city limits. I then walked to the Ohio turnpike. He also shared a sandwich with me. I was hungry by then. It was getting dark and as the sun went down, I realized I could not hitchhike or walk along the Ohio turnpike without being stopped by the state trooper and perhaps being arrested. I stood near the entrance to the Ohio turnpike and put my thumb up, hoping someone would give me a ride. As it got later and later the temperature dropped further, I became very cold. Around one thirty or two o'clock in the morning, a young man in a car stopped. He asked if I wanted a ride and I definitely wanted one and appreciated the fact that he had stopped. He was in the military and was traveling by himself. After a while he asked me if I would drive, which I was glad to do. He was not going to Cleveland, but he was going in that general direction, and I was extremely cold, so I was glad to get any ride.

I drove into the night and he slept until about sunrise. It began to warm up and I explained to him that I was actually going to Cleveland and not Cincinnati or wherever his destination was. I thanked him for the ride, and he dropped me at the next rest stop, past my destination of Cleveland. I bought a cup of coffee, got my bearings and started to walk back in the direction of Cleveland.

After walking most of the day I arrived near a suburb of Cleveland where I could board a suburban bus. I arrived in Cleveland late that evening about dark. The trip between Detroit and Cleveland by automobile was about a four-hour trip. My trip took approximately thirty hours. Once in Cleveland, I had no place to go. At that time, the only people I actually knew in Cleveland were Mr. and Mrs. Robert (Helen) Freeman from whom I rented a room in a rooming house in 1953. After looking up their phone number and calling them, no one answered the phone. I spent my first return night to Cleveland on the city park bench down near Public Square.

In order not to be arrested for loitering, I slept for an hour or two, then went to the train station and sat there; then I went back to the street for a couple of hours and to the bus station for an hour and to get warm; then I returned to the street. The train station and the bus station provided me with warmth and toilet facilities and a deviation from city park benches. They were approximately fifteen blocks apart and I had no difficulty walking between two locations and taking advantage of the facilities that were open to the public.

E.J. Nichols had a friend in Cleveland who worked for the Department of Economic Security and through that contact; I was able to register for work at a day labor center. Unfortunately, most of the jobs that they assigned were in the suburbs of Cleveland. I found myself spending bus fare out to the suburbs to do work. We were usually compensated with a check after all the banks and facilities were closed. As money was tight, I found myself walking more and more between the downtown Cleveland area and the suburbs. What monies I did make, I tried to send home to Delphine and the children so that they would have money for food and other necessities. This kept me on the street. After about a week, I walked to the Cedar Avenue YMCA, a Friday night, and rented a room for two dollars. I had a total of three dollars at the time. The other dollar was put up as a key deposit. My plan was, after I checked out the next morning; I would use the dollar for food. Since I had not been in a bed for such a long period of time and was so tired, I didn't awake until Sunday morning. I was panicky because I knew I had slept two nights and that I had forfeited my key deposit in addition to owing another dollar. When I went to check out, the clerk did not notice or was kind enough not to mention the fact I had slept another day and returned my dollar to me. In all of my upbringing, my desire to be honest and my commitment to the truth were tested that morning when I had to decide whether I would tell the clerk that I had been there an extra day and walk away from my one dollar that I had planned to use for food. My hunger got the better part of me and I took the dollar and went to McDonalds.

In a letter dated August 23, 1962, I advised my family of the experiences I was having as a homeless person in Cleveland.

LETTER (TYPED & COPIED FROM)
FROM FREDERICK E. BOWMAN, SR.

TO: FAMILY IN DETROIT, MICHIGAN
DATED AUGUST 23, 1962

Dear Family,

I hope that this letter finds you all in the best of health. Everything here is going well.

I spent the day looking for a job and things still look good. I am in the public library and can hardly stay awake. I spent the night sitting in the bus station. What an experience! First, I was afraid and thought everyone knew I had no home, but after several hours, I found out that only about 5% of the people in there were waiting for the bus. Most of us were camping.

This morning I used their washing up equipment and got on my way early. I am beginning to believe that this is the age of the homeless man. (Smile) One of the people that I met when I was here before gave me some money and I got my shoes fixed. I really wore them out getting here. Since I don't have enough clothes to make myself look different, I'll sleep in the train station tonight. (Smile) I have to see a woman tomorrow about a permanent job and another on Monday. I am going to start doing day labor tomorrow and should have some money and be headed home soon if you can hold off that long. Everyone here has been swell, and I'm sure we will be OK soon. I dreamed about Vera in the bus station last night. I hope this doesn't mean she is messing with my kids. I'm going to close now and get this in the mail.

Love,
Fred
Kiss the kids for me.
Friday Evening

P.S. The address on 76th Street belongs to friends of mine who are not at home for some reason. In an emergency, contact Mrs. June Moxley -636 E 94th St., Tel No. PO 1-1198

One morning in late August, while using the restroom at the Greyhound bus terminal in Cleveland to clean myself up and change into whatever clean clothing I had taken out of the storage lockers, I noticed that the plumbing in one of the washbasins was broken. After getting my clothes changed and returning my items to the storage locker, I went to the office of the terminal manager. I told him I had skills that would allow me to correct the plumbing and to do other maintenance work around the terminal and asked for a job application. The terminal manager told me that the plumbing in the restroom was not his concern. A contractor, who had a shoeshine stand in the area, also had the responsibility for the maintenance of the restroom equipment. I explained my condition to the manager; that I was a father of three, an army veteran in need of employment, and that I was willing to work and was, in fact, a hard worker. Although he was reluctant to give me an application, I insisted, and he allowed me to complete an application. I put my address as that of the Freemans on East 76th Street and used their telephone number. I continued to use the Greyhound terminal for rest and to use their facilities to refresh myself and clean myself up.

Three days after I had applied for the job, I went back to the offices of the Terminal Manager, who was actually happy to see me, and said that he had made an attempt to contact me. He had an opening for a janitor while the janitor was on vacation for a week. He said that when he contacted the Freeman's telephone number, the person answering the phone had no knowledge of my presence and told him they had not seen me for years, which was true because I didn't even know that the Freemans had returned. I assured him he had talked to someone who was not familiar with the fact that I had returned to Cleveland. I was anxious and took the job for one week as a janitor. All the jobs that were posted weekly in the Greyhound terminal were under the union contract. The opening was not for a janitor, but for a baggage agent, and I was hired as a temporary employee.

Through work as a day laborer, I had accumulated or squirreled enough money to rent a room at a large rooming house on East 69th Avenue. The rented room was in a house with other roomers. The room was furnished with a bed and a small hot plate; with a sink, but no restroom facilities. Those were down the hall and shared by other roomers. The building and the neighborhood were such that when I was outside, I was afraid to enter. When I was inside, I was afraid to remain inside or leave. When I entered or exited, there were paramedics at the entrance or police there, for some reason. I knew that I needed to get out of there as soon as possible.

By now, I was pretty astute at shopping at the Salvation Army thrift store. I purchased one knife, one fork, one spoon, one pot, one frying pan, one plate, one saucer, and I was in business. I went to the store and bought one loaf of bread, a dozen eggs, some lunchmeat, and some mayonnaise. I was in business! The Greyhound bus station in Cleveland was on Thirteenth Avenue. By now I had my shoes repaired from the damage they had suffered in the walk from Detroit and I was able to walk between the bus station and home, and to and from work. In a letter on September 4th, which I didn't mail until after amending it on September 9th, I advised my family that I had worked at the Greyhound Bus Station for five days and would send them a reasonable amount of money on pay day.

LETTER FROM FREDERICK E. BOWMAN, SR.

TO: FAMILY IN DETROIT, MICHIGAN
DATED SEPTEMBER 4 & 9, 1962

My Dear Family,

I hope that this letter finds you in the best of health and spirit. Everything is going well here with me. I worked 5 days at the Greyhound Station and I'm off today and tomorrow. I hope to find a permanent job during this time. Two people tried to contact me about jobs, but Mrs. Freeman, the lady here on 76th St. didn't know where to find me. I am giving up my room here on 69th St. today. First because of money (smile)... got none, second Mrs. Freeman said I could stay there until I get organized. I called mother yesterday and she told me she had been helping you out. I was glad you are getting help, but sorry we had to ask her for it. (Don't ever let her see this) Maybe one day, we will get organized and can quit begging for help all of the time.

Have you heard anything from Vera? I am sure that mother and the family have said I'm a dog for leaving the way that I did. I'll be living at Mrs. Freeman - 2262 E 76th St., Cleveland ,Ohio, if you should need to reach me for anything. I may come home on the weekend to get some clothes and my tools; this seems to be the only way to get them. I suppose Dr. Nichols has left for Kansas.

SEPTEMBER 9, 1962

My Dear Family,

I hope that this letter finds you all in the best of health and spirit. Everything is going well here with me. Today is Sunday, and I was trying to get the things that the lady brought over for me. I'm going by later after she comes home from church and get them. I am sending you $13.00. I owe Mother three ($3.00) that she sent me. If you need it, use it and tell her I'll send hers next week with some money for the phone bill, if you can spare it to her (offer it to her). Friday I'll send you at least $65.00. Give Mrs. Mehoney $50.00 on rent and maybe you can get by on what is left. I am not sure how long this job will last, but I'll stay as long as I can. I hope to bring the children (move) over here by the end of the month. I suppose you can't come until the baby is born. I would have sent you more money, but my shoes were worn out and so were my pants. I brought some and they will have to make it until Friday. I wish you would write sometime so I wouldn't be so worried all the time. The only thing that it does when I'm not told about what is going on is to get worried half to death.

I have slept about 13 hours in the last 4 or 5 days. I'll be OK if someone tells me what is going on sometimes. It was nice to hear about the kids and I wish I could see them. Tell Denise and Monique to take care of their doll babies.

Thanks for everything that you are doing for the kids and me. You have made a friend that will never forget. I'm not going to be poor all of my life and when I get straight; I'll remember you and help you. I am going to close now and will write again before Friday.

Love,
Fred

The good news was also that I was able to move out of the room on Sixty-Ninth and move over in a place on Seventy-Sixth where Ms. Freeman had welcomed me to stay until I got organized. My one week of temporary work at the bus station was extended to two weeks, three weeks, and months and only ended in June 1964. I was accepted in supervision and transferred to Detroit, Michigan as city sales representative for Eastern Greyhound lines. When I began with Greyhound in Cleveland, there were a limited number of Negro employees, most of whom were red caps, and janitors. I learned I was one of the first to work as a baggage agent and as an express agent.

Each week under the union contract, jobs were posted and bid on seniority. Since I was the last person to bid, I found myself on the midnight shift, which started at 12:05 a.m. and ended at 8:35 in the morning. I was able to bid into the express room, which had been exclusively white, because I had the ability to perform the assignment with limited training; the assignment was left open at the end of all bidding. Greyhound didn't pay a lot of money at that time. It was steady work with benefits after you finished your probation period, and with an opportunity for advancement to a higher-paying position. My family, who lived in Detroit, and I were extremely pleased that I had been able to find stable work. Now, I was in a position to look for a place for them. When I brought them over to Cleveland, Mrs. Freeman with whom I was staying, had moved from the rear house, remodeled the front house and made it her home.

There was space available in the rear house for roomers at that time, although there were no vacancies.

In the third week that I was in Cleveland, I received an urgent message from Delphine, the children's caregiver and housekeeper, that Child Protection Services in Detroit, Michigan, had contacted her. The Child Protective Services personnel informed Delphine that they had received advice from one of my family members that I had abandoned the children, and that they were coming to investigate. Delphine was concerned that Child Protective Services would come in my absence and take the children away from her. The only available vehicle to me at that time belonged to Mrs. Freeman. She generously agreed to loan me her automobile, a Buick 225, which was in excellent condition; she allowed few people to drive her car.

That following weekend, I drove to Detroit, Michigan, and packed up the children and all their personal belongings in the car. I left Delphine in the flat until she could locate sufficient living facilities and I returned to Cleveland with the children and their personal belongings. The children and I lived in one room of the house where Mr. and Mrs. Freeman made their home for a few weeks, until space became available in the rooming house in the rear. I returned to Detroit as soon as possible with a rental truck and moved the furnishings that I had accumulated in the flat back to Cleveland and stored them until I had a place where the children and I could establish a new home. I continued to work at Greyhound, mainly at night, and to use the daytime to seek out and do maintenance work, wherever I could.

We moved the furnishings and the children in the first floor of the rear rooming house and set up housekeeping. I then assumed responsibility for providing babysitting and housekeeping for the children in that we were in separate quarters from Mr. and Mrs. Freeman. Mrs. Freeman and her husband continued to be extremely helpful and continued to provide assistance, by baby-sitting and watching out for the children when I needed their assistance and when they were available. Just like it was when I lived in Detroit, I continued to pay much of my income for child-care services.

Unable to create enough income from my job at Greyhound and from doing maintenance work to cover the costs of caring for the children, paying rent, buying food and clothing, medical costs and childcare, I began to look for a second job. I interviewed and was hired at a small plant in East Cleveland, approximately 20 minutes from downtown Cleveland, by way of Rapid Transit. My initial employment was driving a 2-½ ton truck throughout metropolitan Cleveland and surrounding suburbs, but as far away as Akron, Canton, and Youngstown. Since I worked 5 nights a week, most times, I was driving a truck on little or no sleep. When I reflect back, I realize how dangerous this situation was. In fact, I was but a lethal weapon on the Ohio highways and streets.

The plant where I worked had quite a bit of machinery and plumbing, which often broke. I had also observed that the management did not closely supervise the employees that worked there. On many occasions, they almost stole as many items as we produced during the day. The factory used a large amount of sugar, in that it manufactured sundries, syrups and other items that required sugar. I observed the employees leaving the plant with the back of their car so loaded with 100lb bags of sugar that they could not get down the curb without the bumper dragging. I approached the management of the plant and suggested that they hire someone else to drive the truck, and that they let me come into the plant as a hands-on lead person who would also provide some of the repairs and maintenance that they needed.

They hired a man as a truck driver who surprisingly enough was approximately 45 years-old and lived with his mother. This was his first job. I remember him reporting to work on the first Monday that he was to take over the truck, wearing pointed toe alligator shoes and dress slacks. We helped him load the truck. Within a half hour, we received a report that he had wrecked the truck at the first intersection from the plant.

As I continued to work in the plant, I observed a man who occupied a small office in the rear of the plant yet was not involved in the plant's day-to-day activities. I determined that he had a substantial amount of authority over the plant and appeared to be a businessperson with activities outside of the plant. On an occasion, I introduced myself to him. His name was James Ullman, and he was very cordial. We established a relationship. I learned that Mr.

Ullman was a real estate investor who owned large amounts of property throughout metropolitan Cleveland.

After working on many of the machines and other items in the plant, I approached Mr. Ullman about doing some work on some of his properties. He was agreeable and provided me with whatever amount of maintenance work I could handle, in addition to working 5 nights a week at Greyhound as a baggage and express agent, and working 5 days a week, 8 hours a day in the plant. My schedule at that time was, I would go to work at Greyhound at 12:05am. I would complete that shift at 8:35am, having had a half hour lunch break.

I would literally run from the Greyhound Bus Station to the Rapid Transit Station in the Terminal Tower Building in downtown Cleveland (approximately 14-15 blocks). I would board a train that took me to East Cleveland and transfer to a bus that took me to the plant. I started to work at the plant at 9:00 or 9:15 am. I worked 8 hours at the plant and finished at 5:30 pm. I then proceeded to one of Mr. Ullman's properties and to do whatever maintenance work I could in the evening hours, which were generally done inside. If and when I had a day off from Greyhound, or was not working in the plant, I used that opportunity to perform maintenance work at one of Mr. Ullman's properties. In between these activities, I shopped for groceries, went to the Laundromat, ironed clothes, and spent whatever time I could with the children; and on occasion, I slept. Often, I would go through my cycle of four or five days without ever lying in a bed.

As I began to perform more and more work for Mr. Ullman on his properties, we became better acquainted, and he became familiar with my plight. On an occasion, I spoke to him about not having a vehicle that would allow me more flexibility in moving between the two jobs and maintenance assignments. Although he reminded me that he was not in the banking business, he agreed to make a contact for me, which would allow me to obtain a loan and purchase an automobile. Mr. Ullman told me to go to Cleveland Trust Bank Branch on 97th Avenue and Euclid in Cleveland, and to ask for a person by name. My credit was still seriously impaired or non-existent. Therefore, I did not know what to expect when I arrived at the bank. I realized that there was no way I could withstand a credit check at that time.

When the man came out of his office after being informed by the receptionist that I was there to see him, he approached and called me by name. He informed me that Jim Ullman had told him that I was coming down. He said, "How much money do you want?" I could hardly believe my ears. I said I would like a loan of $1,500. He asked, "How would you like it. Would you like it placed in a checking account or do you wish it as cash?" Since I had already shopped for a used Chrysler 300 that I would be able to purchase for $800, I told him that I would like $1,000 in cash and $500 in a Cashier's Check. He immediately returned to his office and returned with a small-completed form, which included my name and the amount of money I owed, the Cashier's Check and the cash. He told me what the payment would be and when it was due, had me sign the document, thanked me, and I left. I immediately realized what type of buying power and influence Mr. Ullman had.

I was excited when I arrived home. It was in the winter. There was snow on the ground, and I had been struggling, trying to move between the two jobs and perform the maintenance work. I told Mrs. Freeman that I now had the funds to purchase an automobile and I asked one of the people who lived in the rooming house if he would take me to pick up the car. Mrs. Freeman's Buick car was parked in the driveway in front of the vehicle that was to be used to take me to pick up my car. I asked Mrs. Freeman if she would move her car. She said, "Here is the key, go ahead and move it yourself." I had driven the car to Detroit, Michigan, and I had driven her to various places on many occasions. I was excited … I was going to get some transportation. It appeared that my luck had started to change.

I had a friend; I also had some money over and above the cost of the car. When I started the car, I noticed that it was idling fast, but did not think much about it. I placed the car in gear, and it started back without my foot on the accelerator. I reached for the break and hit it, on which the car fired backward at a high rate of speed, striking a street-light pole on the other side of the street, which broke off and fell through the windows of a home across the street. My joy was short-lived. Not only was I in a position where I was going to have to pay for her car, I also had to repair the front of the building across the street and I knew the City would come after me for the light pole.

With my maintenance experience, I was able to repair the damage to the house, replace the window, paint it and make whatever other adjustments were needed, paying only for the cost of materials and my time. I could not replace the street-light pole, which the City came out and worked on. I remember watching them do that; they had two vehicles with trailers and a crew of approximately 6. They stood, they talked, they worked a little and it took approximately 8 hours. I later received a bill from the City for well over $1,500 that included waiting time and extra items. I protested and thought that the fee was outrageous yet paid it after they attempted to impound my vehicle and driver's license. Mrs. Freeman informed me that her insurance would not cover me; therefore, I ended up paying for repairs on her car, which were substantial. I was broke again. Even worse, I was an additional $1,500 in debt to the bank and still owed money for the repair of her Buick.

The purchase was made for the used Chrysler 300 from the monies that I had received. I had it tuned up and it provided me with some service. One night on little or no sleep, I was traveling from the house on 76th Avenue to Greyhound, which was on 13th Ave via Central Ave in Cleveland. I didn't remember anything after 55th Avenue, until the collision at 30th Ave, wherein I struck a vehicle while asleep and drove through a red light. No one was hurt. I assume because I was asleep, my foot was not heavy on the accelerator, but the damage to both vehicles was substantial. During the police investigation, I convinced them that my brakes had failed. Their check revealed that they were working at the time. I received a ticket and assumed liability for damage of both vehicles.

I was still married at the time and I had no idea where Vera was, but I knew that she was providing no child support or other funds to the family. Now I was under the burden of the bank loan, the repairs to the telephone pole, Mrs. Freeman's Buick, my Chrysler and the vehicle that I had hit in the intersection. Out of desperation, I was able to convince a female friend of mine to accompany me to the offices of Household Finance and to act as Vera Bowman when we applied for a loan. Obviously, our charade was successful. Household Finance loaned us money, and I was able to pay off some of my bills. —

My life was moving extremely fast, especially between worksites and with little rest. The Chrysler was no more than 6 months in my possession when I was driving down the freeway heading to work at the plant from my nightshift at Greyhound when I heard a loud noise and realized that I had "thrown a rod." The car was then worthless, although I had already had the bodywork done on it from a previous accident. I was able to drive the car to an exit and happened to pull the car off at the location of a Ford dealer.

I had no money, limited income, great indebtedness, but I had a great imagination and creativity. I went into the dealership and a sales-clerk was very anxious to assist me. He showed me many vehicles of which one was a new Thunderbird. He assured me that he could get me in the car, to which I questioned, "Can you keep me in it?" He expressed surprise that that would be my concern. I took him outside and showed him the Chrysler, and then asked him about a trade in for which we arranged $50 towards the down payment for a 1963 Ford 500 Coupe. I very promptly took out my checkbook and wrote him a check for $300 knowing full well that it probably would not have been a good check if I had written it for only $3. Through some creative financing, I covered the check. I completed an application for financing, in which I created an entirely new identity for myself based primarily on my correct name, address, date of birth and social security number, but lacked information about my past credit and recreating my work record.

Although I had only been working in the plant approximately 6 months, I gave myself 3 years seniority in the plant. I then proceeded to the plant where I intercepted Mr. Ullman who had been my lifesaver on many occasions. I explained to him that I had purchased a new car and what had happened to the other one. I told him that I had used him as the name of my employer rather than the Plant Manager, who unfortunately, was not supportive of my condition. He immediately told me, "Fred, as much as I like you, I will not lie for you." "Mr. Ullman," I said, "I would never ask you to lie." With a smile on his face, he then asked what I wanted him to do. I said, "Mr. Ullman, if my estimation is correct, when they call you, the conversation will probably be that Mr. Bowman came in and made application and said he worked there for 3 years, or words to that effect." I said, "Don't lie. In an indignant manner say, 'What did he tell you?' After which simply say to him, 'Well' and if that does not work, I will think of something else." The telephone conversation played out just as I thought, and my application was so creative that the dealership was impressed, and they put the credit through with Ford Motor Company with a lower interest rate.

The following weekend, while sitting at a stop sign and before I received the new license plates, with Mrs. Freeman in the car, a person under the influence of alcohol ran into the rear of the new Ford. "I'm going to buy you a taillight lens," he said in a drunken voice. The taillight lens was the only thing on the rear of the car that wasn't damaged. Mrs. Freeman stopped me before I could beat the hell out of him. After much effort, I was able to collect most of the money for the repairs.

Fellow employees at Greyhound were both impressed and envious of my new car. One employee went to the Manager and told him that I had a second job. I was always anticipating trouble in that I had so much experience in it. I made sure that I performed more work than anyone on either of the two jobs and I dared anyone to question my productivity. The Terminal Manager, Mr. Clemens, approached me one day and said, "I understand you work a second job." Why are you asking?" I said. "I need to know," he said. "Why?" I said. "I just need to know," he said. My response was, "I do as much or more work than any person you have in this job classification. No one has ever questioned my productivity. I do a satisfactory or above satisfactory job for you. What I do when I am not here is none of your business. Please don't ever ask me about it again".... and he never did.

Working 40 hours a week at Greyhound, working in the plant 40 hours a week and performing maintenance work, along with taking care of the children, allowed me little time for sleep or any other activity. It took its toll on me and I found myself not only tired, but also passing out on occasions. There were times when I would stand at the Greyhound Express counter conducting business in the middle of the night and I would completely black out and fall to the floor. Knowing that this would upset customers and they would report that I was possibly ill or something, I very carefully placed items on the floor around where I worked. When I hit the floor, I always woke up. I immediately grabbed the paper, pencils and other items off the floor and sprung to my feet immediately shocking the customers. "Are you OK?" was always the question to which I answered, "I am fine. I was simply picking up something." There were debates as to whether I had passed out or whether I was picking up something, but no one ever reported the fact that they had observed me passing out.

There was an occasion when my mother came to Cleveland, primarily to attend a session of the National Baptist Convention. She brought a friend of hers with her. I told mother and her friend that they could stay with us in our small quarters. I gave up my bed, which I did not occupy very much, so that they would have my bedroom. I picked my mother up at the Greyhound Bus Station, upon her arrival, and took her to my home. I dropped her off and only stayed for about 15 minutes, advising her that I had to go to work. She was somewhat confused in that when I picked her up from the bus station, I told her that I had just gotten off from work. Upon arriving home again at about 8:30 pm, I informed my mother that I had to go shopping and to the Laundromat and would be back in approximately 1 to1½ hours. At about 9:00 or 9:30 pm,

I advised my mother that I was going to lie down across the couch and that I needed to be awakened at about 11:00 pm. She asked, "Why don't you get in the bed?" I said, "Because I have to go to work and I need to be up by 11:00." "Please wake me up." When my mother shook me at 11:00 pm, I was in a state of confusion, and fell across the coffee table when I tried to walk. I got up, and then staggered to the bathroom to wash up and change clothes. On my way back, I tripped over a chair and fell again. My Mother said, "What is wrong with you?" I said, "Nothing, I am tired." I walked out on the porch, tripped and fell down the steps. Half crawling I got into my car and buckled myself into the bucket seat. My mother followed me out and asked where I was going, and I told her that I was going to work. She said, "You are in no condition!! You can't even stand up." At this point, I said, "Mother, this is how I live. This is how I take care of the children. How did you figure that this was being done? I am not a pimp. I am not a thief. No one is giving me anything, and I pay for all of the services that I get. The only way that I can do that is by working, working, and working.   Now please go back into the house and let me go to work." As my mother backed away from the car, I reached under the bucket seat, took out a pint of rum, took a drink and replaced it under the seat. I left the house and reported to work at 12:05am for my Greyhound shift.

I stopped by my house the next morning, on my way to the plant, and my mother told me that it appeared that I needed some help and that she would stay over for a couple of days so that I would not have to pay a babysitter. My mother returned to Detroit after spending three days with us and I continued my activities as usual. I went back to working as many as 4 or 5 days without going to bed and then collapsing on the fourth or fifth day and sleeping for some time. No other family member ever visited the children and me when we lived in Cleveland between 1962 and 1964.

By the fall of 1963, Jim Ullman and I had developed a strong relationship and he trusted my ability to perform many maintenance tasks. He suggested that we purchase some properties together, with him handling the finances and me doing the remodeling, and that we sell them for profit, after they were completed. Our first and only venture was the purchase of two 2-family flats that were next door to each other.   They were nice 3-bedroom units but needed much work inside and outside.   The plant manager was aware of my rigorous work schedule and said one day that he was afraid that I was going to die in his plant and sue him. Although I had performed many services for the plant both as a worker, maintenance and lead person, he evidentially did not appreciate my value.

On an earlier occasion, they had purchased a piece of equipment that was designed to automate the manner in which they filled milk cartons and gallon jugs. The device that an engineer built had six nozzles and was programmed so that it would dispense a half-gallon or gallon amount from each of the 6 nozzles. When they received this device, they hung it from a support over a conveyer line. They had three people to stand around this devise and hold one container in each hand up to the nozzle, while the fluid was being dispensed. I advised them that I was capable of devising something that would be much more efficient, and that would require fewer workers.

Using my experience as a maintenance person, I went to the junkyard and picked up some materials, which included weights, pulleys and other devices. I then designed racks that would hold the six cartons in a position where the people had held them in their hands. The devices were then placed on a conveyer, which I lined up with the six-headed dispensing devices that they had the engineer build. Using pulleys and counter-weights, I arranged for the device to drop down onto the cartons or gallons that came forward on the conveyer and stopped in the exact location; wherein one operator could press a button and all 6 cartons or jugs could be filled. That carrier, with the six cartons or jugs, would then be moved forward, followed by a second, third, fourth and fifth device. One person could now operate the entire conveyer, eliminating the need for two people. For this and other innovative ideas around the plant, I received no additional compensation.

I took every opportunity to work on the two houses that Mr. Ullman and I had purchased. In an effort to expedite their completion, and in an effort to obtain my portion of the profits from the project, I needed some help. Although I was able to do much of the work, my working full time at Greyhound and providing other maintenance services limited the amount of time that I could work on the houses. I purchased additional tools, including a floor sander that allowed me to provide more services.

Before entering the service, I had made the acquaintance of a young man that my brother, Kenneth, had befriended who was being raised by a single mother. This young man had maintenance skills and was able to perform much of the work on the houses that needed to be done. I contacted him in Detroit and arranged for him to come to Cleveland, Ohio. He brought with him a cousin with whom I was also acquainted. It had been approximately 5 years since I had had any contact with this young man, but I still felt that he would be able to assist me. When he arrived in Cleveland, we were able to expedite work on one of the houses during the first week. On the second week of work, and after I had advanced him some money, he went on a drinking binge, which included his consuming a large amount of 151 proof rum. That weekend, he went berserk and destroyed much of the repair work that we had done to one of the houses. After assessing the damage, I immediately took him to the Greyhound Terminal, placed him and his cousin on a bus, and they returned to Detroit. Within a month, I received word from Detroit that both of them had been involved in a heated argument and the cousin shot my friend to death.

It was a cold winter day and I was at Mrs. Freeman's home on 76th Avenue when I met a young man who was looking for something to eat, clothing to wear and a place to stay. All of the utilities were on at the houses where I was doing the repair work and I had space for someone who needed to get in out of the cold. I gave him some of my clothing, took him to the house and gave him a place to stay. He said that he was looking for work, but every time I came from work and every time I encountered him in or around the house, he was doing nothing but sleeping or listening to the radio or reading. I tried to get him to help me with my project, but he said that he didn't have any skills such as carpentry, electric or basic maintenance. However, I soon learned that it was not lack of skill, but lack of initiative or ambition that kept him from doing anything.

After two weeks, I asked him to move out because he was costing me money by using the utilities. In addition, I no longer trusted him. I left him in the house when I went to work at Greyhound one night, only to return to find both the front and the back door of the house standing wide open and many of my tools and other personal items missing. The police told me that there was nothing that they could do, except complete a theft report. One of the officers gave me his card and said that if I were to locate him, I could call him, and he would arrest him. I felt extremely betrayed, in that I had very little to lose at that time and the setback from my friend doing damage to the house and this young man stealing many of my tools and my personal belongings, questioned my desire to help others and to trust.

One evening I made it a point to visit any place in and around the neighborhood where I had met the person who had stolen my property. I found him in a restaurant and immediately sat down beside him in a booth blocking his exit. I suggested that he not try and leave in that I would do bodily harm to him to whatever extent necessary to keep him from leaving. I called the server over, gave her the card and coins, and asked her to call the detective and tell him that I had this person in my possession and that I wanted him arrested. The police arrived shortly and arrested him. Much to my dismay, they let him plead to a lesser charge and sentenced him to probation and community service without any restitution for the items stolen.

I took every opportunity to take a break to be with the children, take them to the movies, circus, church and the park. Many times, I covered the paint on my body with clothing, knowing that I would return to work as soon as I dropped the children off. We completed the repairs on the insides of the houses; decorated both inside and out and built fences around them. The houses were then placed on the market and sold. Unfortunately, through advances, I had used much of the profit to pay for the care of the children and to provide for their needs.

While working at Greyhound one evening, I observed what appeared to be a supervisor on a bus that was called a freighter. A freighter was a bus where the seats had been removed and the bus was loaded from end to end with Greyhound Package Express shipments. I questioned someone who was also observing the bus as to who that person was. They told me that it was an Assistant Regional Manager. I thought it interesting that he had taken it upon himself to climb aboard this freighter and was throwing packages around and handling the shipments. This seemed like unusual behavior for an Assistant Regional Manager.

In the spring of 1964, I became acquainted with an Assistant Terminal Manager in the Cleveland, Ohio terminal who was about the same age as I. When I was not too busy working, and when he had time, we talked about life, work, the military, and world affairs. We found that we had much in common and we became friends. My new friend was soon promoted to Terminal Manager in Akron, Ohio. Shortly before departing for Akron, he told me that as Terminal Manager he would now have possession of Greyhound's exam that they were using to qualify supervisory applicants. As an employee of Greyhound, I had a pass that would allow me to ride the bus free. My friend said that as soon as I got an opportunity or a day off, I should come to Akron and he would administer the Supervisory test for me without the knowledge of other Greyhound personnel in Cleveland or the General Office of Eastern Greyhound Lines, which was in Cleveland, Ohio.

Shortly after that, I traveled to Akron and took the Supervisory examination, which he forwarded to the personnel department for grading. He called me within a week and told me that I had scored extremely high on the examination and that I should move forward with requesting a supervisory position. I wrote a letter to the personnel department, where I explained that I was a single parent with three children and that I was desirous of supervisory position. I explained to them that such a position would assist me in that I would have normal work hours and have more time to spend with the children. When the Assistant Regional manager that I had seen on the bus reviewed my application and letter referring to needing a regular work schedule to allow more time with the children, he forwarded it with remarks that it appeared that I didn't want to work or want special consideration.

I also forwarded a resume of my military experience and my prior work background. My test score was such that it drew a great deal of interest, and I received interviews shortly after that. Before my application, I knew of one other person in Cleveland or the vicinity around Cleveland working for Greyhound who was Negro and who had been considered for supervision. That person was a Red Cap in the Cleveland Terminal who I understood had taken the test and scored very high, much to the surprise of the personnel there, and people in the general office. He was offered a job as an Operations Supervisor (Dispatcher). It is my recollection that he was in training at the time that I made application.

The Vice-President of Marketing for Eastern Greyhound Lines had a son who worked summers in the terminal and was a college student concerned about being drafted during the Viet Nam War. He and I became friends and I gave him some advice on how to stay out of the war area by using his educational background to apply for the Army Language School in Presidio, California. Upon being drafted into the service, he followed my advice and was admitted to the language school. He learned Russian and stayed away from the war zone. The Vice President of Marketing remembered what I had done for his son and had thanked me on several different occasions.

In June 1964, I was offered a supervisory position with a choice of becoming City Sales Representative for Eastern Greyhound Lines in Detroit, Pittsburgh, and New York City. Being familiar with Detroit, having been raised there, and having some family there, I chose Detroit, Michigan, for my first supervisory assignment. Greyhound's offer was that I could have the position, which paid $475 per month, provided I made arrangements to move myself and my family to Detroit at my expense. Still short on money, I visited my friend, Jim Ullman, and told him that I had this opportunity to go into supervision in Detroit. Jim was a small man in stature, but big in heart. He congratulated me on surviving with the children that long as well as the opportunity for promotion into supervision. I explained to him that I needed to move the family back to Detroit, but that I had limited funds. Being the kind gentleman that he was, he told me to go back to the banker that he had referred me to earlier and that he would loan me whatever monies I needed in order to make the move. With the loan from the bank, I packed up the children and rented a trailer for the move. With the help of Gamwell, my friend and "close brother," I moved our belongings back to Detroit. I was unsure how my new assignment with Greyhound would work out in Detroit.

THE BOWMAN FAMILY PHOTOS

Fred & Wilda Bowman in Laughlin, NV on their 41st Wedding anniversary.

Lt. Bowman received 6 of the first 106 Recoilless Rifles Shipped to Europe.

Fred & Gamwell, his close friend who is now deceased, relax With their pet.

*Lt. Bowman & E.J. Nichols (right) dining at the restaurant
of the Berliner Funkturm in 1956.*

Fred & Wilda Bowman dining in Paris, France In 2002.

Fred Bowman working in his office,
The Greyhound Corporation in Chicago, Illinois.

Fred Bowman's Family Picture taken on Christmas In 2008.

*Lt. Bowman, Mess Officer, Berlin Consolidated Mess Hall
at his desk in 1955.*

Monique, Fred, Wilda & Denise.
Their First Christmas morning together in 1969.

The Training Staff, Berlin NCO Academy in Picture taken
by Lt. Bowman - 1956.

William & Flora Bowman with their 6 children in 1939.

*Fred Bowman instructing young Greyhound supervisors
In Cleveland, Ohio - 1974.*

Denise Monique & Fred enjoy a celebration with Family in Berlin in 1967.

Shirley, Fred, Annie, Florence & Violet (seated) as Fred Bids "Good Bye" to his marketing staff in 1968.

Fred & Wilda Celebrate Virginia's birthday with her husband George Steptoe (her parents).

Fred & Wilda visit the Tokyo Tower, Tokyo, Japan in 1980.

Fred & Wilda at Wedding Reception in 1969.

Fred's Grandfather (seated) with William Bowman, Sr., second right, 13 years old in front of family home in Arkansas.

Denise, Monique & Fred, Jr. at an Outing in Berlin, Germany with their Grandmothers Bowman & Schwartz in 1966.

Just the Four Of Us, Fred, Sr. , Denise, Monique and Fred, Jr. in 1965.

*Lt. Bowman issuing the Daily Orders at the NCO Academy,
Berlin, German-1956.*

*Lt. Bowman joins a Major in Berlin to welcome Congressman Gerald Ford
from Michigan, who later became President.*

Fred & Wilda's youngest children, Scott & Erika In 1978.

*William Bowman Sr's family, his parents, brothers, sisters,
spouses and their children, Saginaw, MI — 1941.*

CHAPTER 10

I HAVE A FRIEND
– A LOVE STORY

It was a February day in 1969. The temperature was way below zero and the Chicago wind blew through the city. I was working for Greyhound and trying to take care of the foundation of my heart, my three children. They were still living in Detroit and being cared for during the week. During this time, a friend who was a co-worker approached me once again. Her name was Yvette, a very good friend and someone I trusted. Yvette wanted to introduce me to a lady friend of hers and arrange a luncheon date. After her asking a couple of times and me refusing, I finally agreed to meet this friend of hers who was supposed to be a lot like me. This was the same person, the same lady who she wanted to introduce to me in December at a Christmas party that I wasn't able to attend. I didn't have that kind of time because my three children were my main concern then.

I was traveling back and forth to my job with Greyhound, living in Chicago temporarily. My three children were in Detroit, so my heart, soul and mind were miles away from thoughts of dating. My work travel schedule required that I be away from home as many as five days a week from Chicago, while maintaining the love and care of my children in Detroit. I had to do what I had to do, remembering that not too long ago I was a separated, unemployed parent with limited resources. Greyhound had given me a new promotion. At that time, it was difficult being separated from my children. My weekends were important to me since I spent them in Detroit with the children – my real home and family.

Yvette finally convinced me to meet with her friend with the understanding that I would take the two of them out to dinner with my mind and my options open. We arranged to meet at a small restaurant in downtown Chicago named Plato's. The restaurant doesn't exist anymore, but the memories are still fresh. I still have a book of matches from that date. When I arrived at the restaurant, Yvette and her friend were already waiting. Yvette introduced her as a close friend, Wilda Steptoe. I found Wilda to be an attractive woman, but at that time, my main concern was the survival of me and my children. This took up all my weekends. With my new position as Director of Special Markets for the Greyhound Corporation, I worked hard and managed to hire a weekly housekeeper, Diane, who kept the children during the week. She was the sister-in-law of the family that rented the upstairs flat, and so the arrangement was mutually beneficial. I had an ongoing agreement with the children that I would spend each weekend with them. I agreed that I would be in the house when they awoke on Saturday morning, and I would put them to bed on Sunday evening. As difficult as it was, I kept this arrangement. I would sometimes get caught as the sun was coming up, and sometimes I would be hurrying in from the airport just hours before they awakened. Sometimes I had to try to get out of the house early on Sunday, due to a departure time to some distant point of the country that I had to fly to, be it Boston or Los Angeles.

Yvette, Wilda and I did have dinner that night. At the restaurant, Yvette and I exchanged phone numbers and addresses, and like a gentleman, I said I would call her. Some of those calls came on short notice and since she was a single person, her schedule and mine didn't match up as well as I wanted. Wilda was eight years younger than I and that was something to consider, also. I learned that she had been married for a short period and divorced, yet had no children. I, on the other hand, had three children that she had never met. However, during the month of August, our lives were brought somewhat closer together.

During the 4th of July weekend of 1969, a dramatic change happened that affected our relationship. I had gone to Detroit for the July 4th weekend and Yvette's husband, who had family and friends in Detroit, had traveled to Detroit by car. He wanted to be with his family during that holiday weekend. While riding as a passenger, Yvette's husband, Johnny, was killed in an accident. At this same time, Wilda and Yvette were in Miami on a holiday vacation. I left to return to Detroit and had a heart-to-heart talk with my children. I asked my children for a favor. They agreed that I should stay in Chicago and attend the funeral for Yvette's husband. I wouldn't be able to come home that weekend.

Wilda was at the funeral, and after the services, I asked her if she had any plans. She replied that she didn't. We went out to a restaurant for dinner. It just happened to be the Muslims Nation of Islam Restaurant on 69th and Cottage Grove, where we enjoyed a great meal and had a good time that evening. I asked her if she would be interested in getting together the next day and she agreed. We spent the entire Sunday together. I rented a couple of bicycles and we biked around the north side of Chicago and had a wonderful Sunday outing. When I talked to Yvette, she was excited to hear that we had found each other to be interesting. I found that Wilda was an excellent cook. After having dinner with her one evening at her place, we were washing and drying dishes together. I put my large hand in a water glass and broke it, cutting my hands. She treated my hand with first aid ointments and bandages.

Yvette's car was in Detroit after the accident, and she asked me to drive it back to Chicago. It was the 20th of July and a long night's drive that I'll never forget. The night sky was clear, and the moon was full. I remember very well listening to the car radio. The astronaut's historic landing on the moon was something that most people and I will never forget. Once arriving back in the windy city, Yvette informed me that she couldn't drive a standard stick shift. I responded by saying I could teach anyone how to drive a stick shift in two hours. It took just about that time to teach her. She dropped me off at my apartment on the Northside of Chicago and headed home to the Southside. In those two hours she was able to gain enough confidence to traverse the whole city.

Wilda and I had one more date in Chicago before I invited her and Yvette to a weekend in Detroit. I wanted them to meet the family and my children. I went home every Friday to my children from wherever I happened to be. Sometime in early August, I just happened to be in Chicago, and Yvette and her son Johnny, Wilda, and I boarded the Greyhound bus and we headed for my home in Detroit. We arrived in Detroit late that Friday night. By the time we got to the house, the children were sound asleep. I showed the two women to their room, put Johnny Jr. with Fred Jr., the girls had their bedroom, and I had my separate bedroom.

I awakened the next morning to joyful laughter of children coming from the ladies' bedroom. I soon learned that my three children had gotten into the bed with Wilda, had introduced themselves and were having a good time talking, joking and getting to know each other. They had found each other, and they were having fun. Fred Jr. enjoyed the company with Johnny who was about the same age, and they spent the weekend running, jumping and riding their bicycles. Yvette, Johnny, Wilda and I returned to Chicago late Sunday night and I returned to work Monday morning. Later that month, Wilda and I were out, and I asked her if she wanted to get married. Her response was that she didn't know and to ask her again when I came back to town.

Later, I remember Wilda and me returning home from a date. The route to her house took us past her parents' home. While driving past their home, we noticed them standing outside, looking as though they had a problem that they couldn't solve. We stopped, of course, and I was introduced, and learned that her parents were locked out of their house. A burglarproof house at that! I asked her father if he had any tools. He insisted that it was all right and that there was no way to enter. I again asked if he had any tools, and all I needed was a regular screwdriver and a Phillips-head screwdriver. Wilda's father brought me the two screwdrivers from his car. Reaching past the window guard gates, carefully removing a small windowpane frame in the main door, I reached through the space, disassembling the master lock bolt from the inside. I was able to unlock the door from the inside, allowing them entrance to their burglarproof home.

Quietly, Wilda's father asked her what I did for a living and she replied jokingly that I was a second-story man. This was the perfect time for Wilda to tell her parents what I really did for a living, Director Special Markets Greyhound Corporation, and that she had been dating me and wanted to introduce us all. It was about a week to ten days later when I was back in Chicago that I called Wilda and went by her apartment. I asked her again if she wanted to get married, and she said 'yes'. We then made another trip back to Detroit so that we could tell the children that we were going to get married. They received the news warmly, but as most children would be, they were surprised. I explained to them that although we had a great deal of love between the four of us, bringing Wilda into the family would increase the love by one, and make the family even more loving.

We spent the weekend in Detroit with the children and returned to Chicago that following Monday. Shortly after Wilda and I had decided to get married, I made a difficult career move. I was having a hard time dealing with my supervisor, the Vice President of Special Markets. Using a contact that I had made earlier in my career, a friend and then President of the Greyhound-Lines-East division, I made arrangements to return to the division as a director. Creating still another problem, the headquarters was in Cleveland, Ohio. In September of '69, I transferred to Cleveland, which created a real triangle for Wilda, the children and me. Wilda lived in the Windy City, the children in Motown, and I lived in Cleveland on Lake Erie.

I traveled around the country as much, or more, than I did when I was in Chicago. My assignment in Cleveland was Director of Tours for Greyhound Lines East, which encompassed everything east of the Mississippi, from Canada to Key West. My new supervisor was the Vice-President of Marketing. I arrived in Cleveland and shortly afterward he announced that we were going to do a program called 'fast-start-70.' That would take us to every major market that Greyhound had within our division. We started out in Boston in September and visited every major market that

Greyhound had in the East. I had told my supervisor of my intentions to marry, and he said that he would give me the first available time off when we finished 'fast-start-70.' That weekend was October 25, 1969.

The children and I traveled by car from Detroit, Michigan, to Chicago, Illinois, with my father for the wedding. We were married in Chicago in the home of Virginia and George Steptoe, Wilda's parents. Fred Jr., who was eight years old at the time, was my best man. My two daughters, Denise and Monique, were also at the wedding and were witnesses, while my father, Reverend William Bowman Sr., performed the service. Wilda still laughs at the fact that my father didn't know her name and was calling her "Wilma" during the wedding ceremony. We had a small reception in Chicago at Wilda's parents' house that afternoon. Later that evening, we all squeezed in the car and returned to our home in Detroit.

In Detroit, Frieda Schwartz, the mother of my first wife, was at the house and would take care of the children while we went on our honeymoon. After spending Saturday night in a Detroit hotel, Wilda and I went to Niagara Falls in Ontario, Canada. Since I was Director of Tours, I had connections in the industry that Wilda did not understand. We arrived at the Sheraton Hotel in Niagara Falls on a late Sunday. When we arrived, the desk clerk asked if he could help us. I mentioned to him that there should be a reservation for Mr. and Mrs. Fred Bowman. The desk clerk loudly announced that our guest is here. People swarmed us. Wilda wanted to know what was going on and I asked her to relax. The bellhop then took our bags to a private elevator, which took us non-stop to the level where our suite was waiting on the top floor. It was indeed chilly outside, but they had the fireplace crackling and it was beautiful and warm. The suite was decorated beautifully with an arrangement of flowers and fresh fruit. The champagne was iced to a perfect chill.

We spent three days in Niagara Falls, during which time we visited some of the other hotels and discovered other ventures that were associated with Greyhound. Wilda and I were thrilled with the welcome that we received. We were wined and dined by our host. They gave us the "Keys Honeymoon Certificate", which we now have hanging on the wall in our computer room. When it was time to check-out, the hotel manager came to me in an apologetic manner and explained to me that they had to put something on their books, just for the record. He presented me a bill for every bit of five-dollars. Wilda and I also received the royal treatment at the Sheraton Toronto, Ontario. We occupied the honeymoon suite with all the trimmings of a VIP. Our trip to Montreal, Quebec was no less dramatic. Wilda and I received plenty of food, shopping, and tours around the beautiful city. The partying and the hospitality had been unmatched. We visited restaurants and nightclubs. I remember buying a purse for Wilda and purchasing a crisp-new Canadian dollar bill from the bank and placing it in her purse. Thirty years later in Phoenix, Arizona, she showed me the bill that she still had kept from our honeymoon trip. It is a wonderful reminder of our honeymoon in Montreal.

We returned to Detroit from Montreal Saturday night and on Monday, I went to work in Cleveland. Wilda, her three new stepchildren, my former mother-in-law were all-together in the house in Detroit. A couple of weeks later, Mrs. Schwartz went to visit and stay with my mother who had visited her in Berlin years earlier.

Shortly before Christmas in 1969, I rented a house in Shaker Heights, a suburb of Cleveland, Ohio, where I moved my family. We were all united as a family on Christmas. This was the first time in years that my children had a real, loving mother with whom to enjoy Christmas. This time, this feeling was irreplaceable.

I didn't realize that five doors down the street lived Dr. E. J. Nichols, a childhood friend of mine whom I had known throughout my life, and who had been, and would continue to be a significant person in my future life, as well as in the life of my children. The children were happy and enrollment in school turned out to be easy. Life was good. It was amazing how Wilda assumed the role of mother to my children. I remember when I was working in Cleveland and the children and Wilda were still living in Detroit, I would come home as usual on weekends and hear them addressing Wilda by her first name. When I returned for the second weekend, I noticed a great and warm change about the household. The children were now calling her 'Mom'. When Wilda and I got a private moment to talk, I asked her what had happened to cause them to suddenly stop calling her by her first name in such a short period. Wilda had told them that Wilda had moved out of the house and was no longer responding to her first name. After the children had noticed that they weren't getting any response from the first name calls, they had a group meeting and decided to call her 'Mom'. This decision was made from that day forward; and from that time on, until this day; Wilda has always been called 'Mom'. I was amazed at how Wilda filled into the role of 'Mom' for the children, and I am still amazed today at how she accomplished that feat in such a short period of time. By the way, at the time of our wedding, Denise, my oldest, was eleven years old and felt comfortable with Wilda, even though they sometimes looked like they could be sisters.

Wilda assumed full responsibility for raising the children in my absence. She became involved in their schooling. She shopped for them, sewed and made clothing for them, made sure they were involved in the correct activities, helped them with their homework, and was a good mom and buddy to them, which was most important. Wilda helped them make the adjustments early in their young life to become the beautiful people that they grew up to be. We used every opportunity that we could to do family things together in Shaker Heights, from outside activities to coming together as a family, to doing cleaning around the house.

In 1970, Wilda became pregnant and in December of that year, Scott William was born. This was our first child. Even though I was reluctant to have any more children at the time, I realized that it was unfair for me to expect Wilda to raise my three children from a past marriage and deny her children of her own. I was also delighted that Wilda gave me a second son and Fred Jr. was excited that she gave him a brother. Fred Jr. was so ecstatic that he couldn't wait for us to bring Scott home. Fred was disappointed once he learned that his baby brother couldn't immediately share the same room with him. We had to plainly say that Scott was a baby, and as a baby, he needed to be in our bedroom in a crib, a baby's crib. Fred Jr. went along with the program, thinking as soon as Scott got old enough, he could take charge of him. When Scott grew older and we took him out of the crib and got a bed for him, Fred mentioned that he was old enough now to share the room with him. I was still reluctant to put a child in the same room with a ten-year-old, thinking he would soon get tired of Scott and ask that he be removed. Wilda told me to put him in there and Fred would let us know if and when to take him out. Well, that day never came. Fred and Scott shared a room together until Fred completed Cortez High School in Phoenix in 1979 and went on to Arizona State University. One of the amazing things about the boys sharing the room, unlike the girls, I never heard one argument, or one complaint from one about the other. They were close friends and brothers, and still today share that same friendship and relationship that was developed early on in the family when Fred was a ten-year-old, and Scott was just an infant.

We were close to Dr. E. J. Nichols and Denise was old enough to baby-sit. Dr. Nichols had a young daughter that required babysitting and Denise was happy to perform that service for the doctor and his wife.

Denise, the oldest of the three children, had been required to assume many responsibilities around the house and was a responsible eleven-year--old. She also appreciated the extra money from babysitting for Dr. E.J. Nichols, the money she earned that allowed her to buy things for herself. It was also a chance for her to show her Uncle E.J. that she appreciated his caring for her back in Nashville. The children made friends and settled into their new school.

In 1973, Greyhound assured me that they had no intentions of transferring me again soon. We bought a large English Tutor house on the corner of Lomond Boulevard, across the street from Lomond Elementary School, in Shaker Heights, Ohio. I was continuously traveling in my work, along with other responsibilities, so I had asked Wilda to find us a home. Upon returning, she told me that she had found this house that needed some work. When I visited the house for the first time, I looked it over and realized that it had great potential, but that the owner, who was a divorcee at the time, had not maintained it well and had no intention of upgrading or making any improvements to make the house saleable. Although the house was on the market for seventy or eighty thousand dollars, I had the realtor put in an initial bid of twenty thousand dollars. Wilda was extremely upset with me, as was the realtor, but at that time I was in the business of negotiating and figured I could negotiate the price down to something that was reasonable and I that could afford. On the first visit and for several visits, I wrote a thousand-dollar check as earnest money. I raised the bid one thousand each time until I got to thirty thousand dollars. By the time I reached thirty thousand, the owner had no love for me, at all. She would get frantic every time she saw me coming and kept yelling that I couldn't steal her house. What she didn't know was that I was a master at negotiating. I wrote one last check for one thousand dollars. I told her that thirty thousand was the last bid and to make a point, I also told her that if one of my children, who were with us at the time, reached into their pockets to bring out another quarter, I would break their arm to prove my seriousness.

We received a call late that night from the realtor who informed us that we had just bought the house. We still had the house in Detroit, and I didn't want to sell it at the time, so I arranged for a second mortgage on the new house through the Detroit Bus Credit Union where I had become a member in good standing. I used the second mortgage to make the down payment and repairs. We did all the work in the house, including painting it and all other renovating and redecorating of the house, so it kept the cost to a minimum. I tore up the basement floor and rebuilt the entire basement into a fantastic recreation room. We were able to drop the ceiling, panel the walls, put in recessed lighting, and even added a coat-check room and a rest room, all in the basement. I also added a wet bar that would seat twelve people. I brought all of the children into the basement and had them help me work on the remodeling of the basement. The girls would constantly complain when I asked them to hand me tools. Their constant argument was that it wasn't girl's work.

Wilda and I were blessed with the birth of Erika Virginia July 2, 1974. I had driven Wilda to the hospital when she told me that she was having contractions. I let her out of the car and had taken her into the receiving area, and left to park the car, which took me less than ten minutes. I returned to the hospital and one of the nurses asked me if I would like to see the baby? My reply was, "I wasn't interested in looking at babies, how was my wife doing?" She then said, "Your wife delivered the baby, would you like to see the baby?" Erika had been born almost instantly after arriving at the hospital. Erika is our youngest child. She is a special gift from God. Erika was less than a year old when we moved to Phoenix.

Several years later, I returned home from a business trip, only to find Wilda and her mother crying and upset. At the young age of six years old, Erika had been diagnosed as having Cystic Fibrosis, the number one genetic killer of children and young adults. The life expectancy at that time was then thirteen. I asked them to calm down and invited them into the bedroom where we could talk together, yet not in front of Erika. I told them that we were not counting her out as dead and not to let Erika know or feel our fear.

I requested for them to stay in that room until they could stop crying. They weren't going to scare her to death. Two years later, Wilda, Erika, and I were watching television when a program came on about C.F. When the moderator said that it was the number one genetic killer of children and young adults, she turned to us and said, you guys didn't tell me that it was going to kill me. We were lost for words but assured her that she wasn't going to die soon.

Erika, through our love and support, successfully finished Cortez High School and lettered in track four years. She was a leader in school and won many awards. She was student body president, vice president of the freshman class, and junior and sophomore class president. She went on to the university and received her Bachelor of Science Degree from the University of Arizona. In May 2003, Erika married Jeffery Peoples, but the marriage ended in divorce. She celebrated her thirty-fourth birthday July 2, 2008. Erika works full time as a manager in the Health Care Profession; she maintains a home and has an active woman's lifestyle.

At the end of 1974, following contract negotiations, the President of Greyhound Line, Inc. announced that he was transferring me from Cleveland to Phoenix. I moved to Phoenix in March of 1975, leaving Wilda and the children in Cleveland. They moved to Phoenix in June of 1975 after school was out. I had traveled to Phoenix many times for work before Greyhound announced that they were transferring me, but I didn't have any love for Phoenix. Many times, I expressed my displeasure. When I worked in Phoenix in 1973 and 1974, Phoenix, as I saw it, was hot and with little to offer except a lot of dirt and desert. I didn't know anyone who had a house, no one that I could visit. I had spent most of my time during working visits, moving in and out of hotels and resorts. That was the perception I had of Phoenix. With the decision to move to Phoenix, Wilda was also upset because she had seen Phoenix, and didn't find it very attractive at all. I was able to convince her to move with the understanding that we would sell the house in Shaker Heights, keep the house in Detroit in case we did not like Phoenix, so we would have a place to return.

Our oldest daughter Denise completed high school in 1974, at the age of sixteen. Everyone made the move to Phoenix except Denise who was vacillating about the idea of going to college. Denise was very upset with me because I wouldn't agree to send her off to college, to an out-of-state campus. She hadn't determined what her major was, or what she was going to study. There were many good schools around the Cleveland area, including Case Western Reserve, Cleveland State, and many community colleges and other schools of higher education, but Denise wanted to go away to school. Since she would not comply with the rules and wishes of the family that had been established, it was agreed that she should move out on her own. She thought she was grown. She had a job and had located a small apartment. Fred Jr. and I helped her move in. I knew that since I had raised her right, even though she was only seventeen at the time, she would be all right.   In addition, I was still traveling a great deal and was in a position to set my own schedule. I traveled in and out of Cleveland and was able to check on her and visit at my convenience. I wrote a letter to verify that she was emancipated, so she could conduct business for herself while she lived in Cleveland.

When Denise was 18, she called me and told me she wanted to buy a townhouse. She needed to float a loan for the down payment. I assured her that as long as she paid me back, her credit was always good. With the down payment, she bought the townhouse. And, on my next visit I found that she had written, "This house belongs to Denise" in a room that she was painting. She then took me around the house, and showed me all the repairs she had made, and the tools she had used. I reminded her that although she didn't think it as girl's work that there had been a purpose for them helping me in the basement in Shaker Heights some years ago; they knew how to use tools.

When we decided to move to Phoenix, I contacted a realtor. We searched some areas in and around Phoenix for a home and visited many sites. At that time Wilda and the children were still living in Cleveland, and I was now working out of Phoenix. When I had several possibilities, I sent for Wilda to come out and look at some of the homes with me. When Wilda was scheduled to arrive into Phoenix, I was working in the Industrial Relations Department and I was doing a lot of traveling and trouble-shooting for Greyhound and from day-to-day, I wouldn't know where I would be. I basically was on-call to go and put out fires wherever they might break out. The day before Wilda was to arrive in Phoenix, we had a crisis in Philadelphia. It was one that needed my attention. While I traveled to Philly, instead of calling off Wilda's trip to Phoenix, the realtor agreed to meet her at the airport, take her to her hotel, and to show her the sites that I had already seen..

I thought that I would get back to Phoenix within a couple of days. The problem in Philly turned out to be more difficult than I anticipated, and I ended up being there for over a week. Wilda flew to Phoenix, saw the houses, and then flew back to Shaker Heights to the children. When I returned to Ohio, Wilda and I discussed the houses that she had seen, and we agreed on the one to purchase. Strangely enough, we never saw the house together. The realtor flew into Cleveland with the paperwork, and we signed the documents. The house in Phoenix that we bought was a ranch style that was single level. It had four bedrooms with an attached guest room unit like a small apartment. It sat on a corner lot with a large backyard and a diving pool. When the kids arrived ahead of the furniture, we agreed to move into the house instead of staying at a motel. This was their first experience in the new house, sleeping on a new mattress, and enjoying the backyard pool. We kept my mother, a senior, still living in Detroit, in mind when buying the house. She was really the reason why we were sold on this home with a detached apartment where she could stay. Wilda agreed to this, and we would bring my mother to Phoenix. The apartment had its own private entrance separate from the house. We have remained in this house even to the writing of this book.

In 1977 following a visit with us, Wilda's parents, Virginia and George Steptoe, long-time residents of Chicago, IL, moved to Phoenix within a mile of our home. In January 1980, Connie and Tomas Wamble, Wilda's sister and brother-in law and their three children, also moved to Phoenix and located close to us. Denise moved to Phoenix in 1982. Our Phoenix family was then even stronger and more complete. The children had the benefit of loving grandparents and other relatives – we were able to visit and socialize with them often. I now had more family around me.

My relationship with Wilda's parents was caring and strong. I felt as if they were my parents, too, and it remained so during their illness and until George made his transition in 2000 and Virginia made hers in 2006. All of the children are grown up now, and have moved away to their own homes, while Wilda and I now have the pleasure of enjoying the house and pool with spare space to roam and entertain. My mother never made it to the house and never saw the place that Wilda and I had set up for her. My siblings objected to my offer to move mother to Phoenix because of the distance. They thought they would not have access to her. My brother, who was close to me in age, moved her into his home for a short period of time. Then he said that he could not deal with her, and moved her into a nursing home, where she passed away.

Denise married Dr. Michael Brad Bayless in 1983. She attended Arizona State University, received Bachelor's and Master's degrees, and is a Counselor and faculty at Gateway – Maricopa Community College. She is now a divorced mother who owns a beautiful townhouse and has two grown sons - Justin and Jerryd Bayless.

Monique left home at sixteen years-old and moved around to different parts of the country. She moved from Phoenix to Miami, Detroit, Cleveland, Steamboat Springs (Colorado), California, and Prescott (Arizona). She now resides in Amasa, Michigan. She married Daniel Hackett in 1982, had one daughter named Ayla and later divorced him. In 2009 she remarried, marrying Jeff Iwanski.

Frederick Jr. graduated from Arizona State University with a Bachelors of Arts Degree. He has worked as an Executive with IBM, Hewlett Packard and other Information Service companies. He married Claire Pearson in 1993 and they have two daughters, Victoria and Anika.

Scott William received two Bachelor Degrees, a Master's Degree and a Doctor of Philosophy, in Justice Studies from Arizona State University. He is an Assistant Professor at Texas State University and lives in Kyle, Texas. Scott married Rolanda (Tori) States in May 2000, and they have two daughters, Imani and Qwynci.

On the evening of October 25, 2004, the children--Denise, Monique, Fred Jr., Scott and Erika--honored Wilda and me on our 35th wedding anniversary with a celebration and a dinner buffet reception at our home in Phoenix. We were greatly pleased and honored to be able to entertain eighty of our closest friends and relatives. We are proud and thankful for our experiences together and a few years later, planned our fortieth wedding anniversary dinner party in October 2009. The blessings we have received are tremendous; we are blessed and look forward to our next forty years together.

PART FOUR

GREYHOUND:

TWENY-ONE INTERESTING YEARS

CHAPTER 11

ESTABLISHING MY NICHE

Eight years after I had taken one of the worst rides of my life from Fort Smith, Arkansas, to Detroit, Michigan, for my brother's funeral, I swore that I would never take another Inter-city bus in my life, but then I went to work for Eastern Greyhound Lines in Cleveland, Ohio. The job was as a janitor, and it was promised for only a week or two, but to someone that was experiencing a failing marriage and had accepted the sole responsibility for raising three children ages one, three, and four, it was a lifeline.

The memories of that ride on the back of the bus with snuff, spit out of the window by an old black woman and blowing back into my face most of the way to Detroit in March 1954, seemed like ancient history. Even the challenges of Officer Candidate School and the trials that the Army had presented me with during my four plus years of active duty was nothing compared to what I was going through at the time. Working in the foundry and at the post office seemed to have faded from memory. When Mr. Clements, the Terminal Manager offered me the temporary job, I was grateful. I was assigned to work nights, 12:00AM until 8:35AM - but as a baggage agent - not as a janitor. They had given me a test, something that never caused me problems; my score was high, and my geography was good.

In 1962, Baggage Agents were required to load and unload buses, sort baggage and package express, check the storage lockers and work the baggage counter. When I began employment in September 1962, most of the Negro employees at Greyhound in Cleveland were Red Caps or janitors. I recall only one other Negro that worked as a baggage agent at the time. I was a fast learner and had learned early in life that anything worth doing is worth doing right. My military experience also gave me the ability to excel without direct supervision.

The trip between my rooming house and Greyhound was about seventy city blocks, which I walked each day in both directions, as I needed to save all of the money that I could to pay for the children's care.

Believing that the Greyhound work was for only a week, I continued to look for a permanent job during the day. At the end of the first week, I was kept on for a second week, then a third week, and more. The union contract allowed for a bidding process each week for terminal employees like me. I was the last hired and the last to bid for a long time and I got the midnight shift in the baggage department. When there was an opportunity to bid as a Package Express Agent, I did. The work was inside most of the time and paid more because it required more paperwork. In a short period, I was able to perform all the duties of a baggage or package express agent and I never was a janitor.

Greyhound wages were about $2 to $2.50 per hour, depending on the shift and job assignment. This national company provided other benefits including vacation, free transportation for employees and their families, health care, and a pension program – all of which I thought were important. I quit looking for another job after several weeks and concentrated on learning as much as I could about the company and the job. After I moved the children from Detroit, I found out that my wages from Greyhound wouldn't cover our expenses. Mrs. Freeman, my friend and landlord, was assisting with childcare, while other costs such as rent, clothing, food, medical care, transportation and household items kept me in debt.

I answered an advertisement in the newspaper. I took a job driving a two-and-one-half ton truck during the day. I finished at Greyhound at 8:35 AM, ran to the Terminal Tower Rapid Station, boarded a train to East Cleveland, then a bus, and started at the Plant at 9:00 AM or 9:15 AM depending on how well I made the connections. We loaded the truck and I made deliveries and pickups throughout metropolitan Cleveland and as far away as Akron/Canton, Ohio. With the money from both jobs, I was able to keep up with most bills, but the expenses also went up when I had to pay for more childcare while I was working. Between jobs, I spent as much time as possible with the children, went shopping, did the laundry and anything else that was needed. Sleep was the last thing on my list of things that I wanted to do, and sometimes I went four to five days without getting in or near a bed. After a couple of months driving the truck and a few close calls, I convinced the management at the plant to hire another truck driver and to let me assist with supervising the plant. The plant made sundries like syrup, toppings and other things made with sugar. Sugar was also used to make whiskey and could be sold on the black market for cash. I had watched the sugar leave the plant in one hundred-pound bags by the carload as a supplemental income for some employees. I was able to secure the plant and stop most of the thefts. I also made many of the repairs to equipment and improved some procedures in the plant.

For the next several months, I worked at Greyhound at night and the plant during the day. The Greyhound Terminal was an interesting place to work and to learn about people. In a Greyhound Terminal, you were able to see persons in all phases of life and life activities. People came there because they, like me, had no place else to go. They came to greet friends and relatives for visits, weddings, funerals, birthdays and other celebrations. They came or brought people for departures, to celebrations, to attend funerals, leave for the military service, and leave home for the first, second or perhaps the last time. It was a place for joy, a place for shelter, and a place for sadness. You experienced people at their best and at their worst. Many people came to the Greyhound Terminal happy, drunken, helpful, hateful, sad, mad, and sometimes even violent.

One day after telling another express agent that I believed I had seen everything, a drunk walked across the floor, stopped in the center of the terminal, dropped his pants, sat down on a smoking sand urn and took a dump while making loud grunting sounds. The female at the newsstand, a few feet from where he was facing, tried to avoid making eye contact with him or look at his penis, which was hanging over the end of the urn. Upon finishing, he reached across the bench, collected a used newspaper, wiped himself, as two large Cleveland police officers caught him under each arm and dragged him out the door with his pants around his feet and his penis hanging in the wind. I hadn't seen anything like that before!

On my weekdays off from Greyhound and sometimes following both jobs, I performed maintenance work on houses and in apartments. I was able to find enough work in maintenance to quit the plant and work only full time at Greyhound. When some of the employees at Greyhound found out that I had served as an officer in the Army, they couldn't understand why I was working as a baggage or express agent. Since most of them were white, they thought that someone with that much experience, and a veteran as well, could find better work. *They hadn't experienced racism.*

One of the baggage agents, who was working during college summer break, was facing the draft and his father was the Vice President of Marketing. We discussed the service during which I advised him to apply for the Army Language School in Pescadero, California, in order to stay out of the combat area.

Later, a young Assistant Terminal Manager and I became friends and after he was assigned to Akron, Ohio, as Terminal Manager, he offered to administer the Greyhound supervisor's test to me. When the results were received in the General Office in Cleveland, most of the managers were impressed, including the Vice-President of Marketing. I submitted a resume in which I informed them that I was a single father and was attempting to gain a position that allowed me to spend more time with my children. An Assistant Regional Manager thought that I was looking for special treatment and wrote this in my file despite my work record, test scores and interviews being good.

The Vice President of Marketing offered me an assignment in Detroit, Michigan, starting June 14, 1964, as City Sales Representative, which I accepted. The offer was that the transfer from Cleveland to Detroit was made at my expense. Mr. Ullman, a former employer and friend, helped me to arrange a small loan to cover the move. The salary in the new position was only a few dollars more than I was making as a contract employee, but the opportunities were better.

My best friend, Gamwell Simpson helped me make the move back to Detroit. Again, we packed up the furnishings, personal items and the children's things, and brought them back to Detroit. My mother, who recently was divorced from my father, lived alone in the family home, which was four stories, eight bedrooms, and a full-finished basement. She agreed to allow us to move in with her for a while. The challenge was to meet the financial requirements on the income from Greyhound, learn the new job, present a professional appearance and to be a good single parent.

All of the ghosts of the past were still present in Detroit, except for Vera, the children's mother. Old outstanding debts, business failures and my family, who hadn't been much help, were there to greet me. Before the Christmas holidays in 1964, my mother advised me that I needed to pay more for rent and the assistance with the children. I was attempting to buy Christmas presents for the children and keep up with other expenses. When I was unable to meet my mother's demands and experiencing chest pains, I accepted an offer from my friend Dr. E. J. Nichols and I let him take the children to Nashville, Tennessee, for a few months. It was a very hard decision, but one of the only alternatives that I had.

Within a week of their departure, I was admitted to the hospital for extreme exhaustion and remained there for a week. The City Sales Representative in Detroit was the arms and legs of the City Marketing Manager. The Metropolitan Detroit area, which included all surrounding suburbs and the Northeast to Port Huron, Michigan, was in our territory. There were agencies (contract stations) where the bus stopped, where they sold Greyhound tickets, provided bus tours, processed package express and provided additional services to our customers. There were also "letter" agencies that sold tickets, tours and charters on a commission basis. The Detroit Greyhound Marketing department selected, trained and supervised these agents.

I had never read a tariff, never sold a Greyhound ticket or tour. I had a lot to learn in a short amount of time.

My new supervisor, Mr. Joe McQue, the City Marketing Manager, had many years of experience. He was very generous in sharing information and direction with me. There was no formal training program for new supervisors coming into this position, but there were a lot of reference materials. The office also had a very experienced staff of female secretaries and travel agents. My experience dealing with people proved valuable, as I befriended the staff and other employees in Detroit. I asked a lot of questions, read everything that I could find, and observed all of the activities that I could, in order to gain as much information as quickly as I could. The secretaries asked me how I intended to handle the supervision of my agents with very limited experience, in addition to being the first and only Negro in this position. We set up a file for each agency and placed all of the correspondence and reports that arrived in our office before for their visits. Before scheduling a visit, I would review everything in each file. I would make sure that I understood each item and could answer most questions that might come up about the report or correspondence.

Visits traditionally consisted of a review of all items in the file. The agent was asked if they had any problems or questions. Answers were given only if I was sure of the response and if not, notes were made, with a promise that I would contact them with the information within a week. I pledged to handle their problems and assist them with training and sales if they promptly made monetary deposits and wrote reports. I further assured them that I could only provide this type of service if all of my agents kept their part of the agreement. The arrangement worked out well and I became a star with less agency problems and higher sales than other supervisors.

I worked with the female travel agents to set up new tours and increase the membership in Detroit's Tour of the Month Club. I trained the staff of the telephone information room and increased their efficiency. Our general office in Cleveland and other managers around the country became aware of our accomplishments.

I made as many visits to Nashville as possible to visit the children and found that Dr. Nichols was taking good care of them. They had been joined in Nashville by their grandmother, Frieda Schwartz, who E. J. had welcomed in March of that year. I missed the children more than I could stand and August of 1965, I went to Nashville and returned the children and their grandmother to Detroit where I had rented a small apartment. The grandmother returned to Berlin within weeks, so I placed the girls in a Catholic school, and a friend helped me with Fred Jr.

My job experiences were going well but my personal financial problems continued to mount up. The commitment to the job didn't allow me to find additional income. Request for a salary increase was met with rejection, although I was making less than many contract union employees. The Greyhound Pick-up and Delivery agent offered me some part-time work driving a truck in the evenings following work. Around five or six o'clock I would slip into the restroom and change into some casual clothes and drive the truck into the evening and night. The truck had a telephone in it, which allowed me to stay in touch with the children and give them evening instructions.

Some of the holders of old debts found out that I was back in town and demanded payment. In 1963, the IRS came after me and garnished my check for hundreds of dollars for an error made by a person in Cleveland that prepared my 1963 taxes. All of this was around the time that my car was repossessed. I was tired and I was whipped. I withdrew my pension contributions and resigned from Greyhound on September 13, 1965. I became a full-time employee of the Pick-up and delivery Agent at an increase in salary.

CHAPTER 12

TAKING A LEAP OF FAITH

On occasions, I would visit with Mr. McQue and he would tell me that the position was still vacant. On a visit to Greyhound, near the beginning of 1966, Mr. McQue advised me that Greyhound had increased the salary range for the City Marketing Representative position and that he could offer me more money if I wished to return. On February 15, 1966, I was re-employed by Greyhound Lines in the same position. In April 1966, Mr. McQue was promoted to Regional Marketing Manager for the Chicago Region, to which we reported. When I contacted him to express my congratulations, he offered me the position of City Marketing Manager saying that I was the best choice for the assignment. The normal progression during this period was from City Sales Representative to District Marketing Supervisor and possibility into a City Marketing Manager position. Although there were two District Marketing Supervisors in Detroit who were years ahead in seniority, I became the first Negro in the country to be a Greyhound City Marketing Manager on May 1, 1966,

189

After interviewing several candidates, I selected a young man from Windsor, Ontario Canada, to be my City Marketing Representative. My team, led by me and four long-time Greyhound females (Violet, Shirley, Anne and Florence) went to work training him. I wanted him to know as much as I did and to be the best candidate to replace me when I left. Since he was white, I was still the only Negro in the office. On many occasions when we were together, customers and vendors would approach my assistant, assuming he was Mr. Bowman because he was white. Greyhound and other companies did not have Negroes in my position in 1966. In our office, we maintained a high level of customer service, and training, while also increasing our tour operations, ticket sales, package express sales and agency efficiency. We received recognition from the regional and general office. Many of those that we dealt with by telephone and mail had no idea that I was a Negro. It was easy to assume that since all of the known City Marketing Managers were white, so was Bowman. Things were looking up.

When the children wanted to ride their bikes, I would try to use the elevator to bring them down to the ground floor from the apartment, but when kids were playing on the elevator or it was broken, I would carry bikes down the stairs and back up.

Souren Benian and his wife Knarig had been a part of my teenage life. They owned a large cleaning establishment on the border of Detroit and Highland Park, Michigan. I had worked for them when I was in middle school and high school. I learned to use many of the tools that they had around the cleaners and to operate much of the equipment. When I was thirteen or fourteen years old, Mr. Benian asked me if I could drive. My older brother--by eighteen months—Delano, had allowed me to drive the family car three-fourths of a block down the alley behind our home, which was several blocks from the cleaners. I believed that this qualified me as a driver, so I replied, yes. He gave me the keys to his 1949 Oldsmobile 88 and sent me on an errand. He trusted me. I returned safely and continued to drive his car, his brother's cars and the company truck until I was out of high school and left the company.

Although the Michigan MVD required that you be sixteen before you could get a permit of any kind. Mr. Benian and I had an understanding that in case of an accident, I should call him, and he would arrive and take care of it. When the brakes failed on the older Ford truck and I had a minor accident, he came out and took care of the damage to the other car and then bought a new truck for me to drive.

He had two young sons that spoke no English, only Armenian. He said that they would learn English later, but if they didn't learn Armenian before going to school, they wouldn't learn it. On many occasions, they would trust me to chauffeur the children. The Benians were protective of me and treated me as if I were family. Maintaining contact with people that were (and are) important to me has always been one of my personal, major objectives. I would go back and visit the Benians often after I finished high school, when I went into the service and returned. Mr. and Mrs. Benian owned a two-family flat on the northwest side of Detroit, of which I was familiar. I had performed some repair work on the home years before. He offered to sell me the house on a Land Contract, with a small down payment and a promissory side note. In addition, he agreed to leave some of the furnishings that we needed in the house. I was still strapped for cash, had very little savings and could come up with all but $300. I contacted my father, a retired International Representative for The United Automobile Workers (UAW), C.I.O, divorced from my mother, remarried and asked him for a $300 loan. He said that he didn't have it, which was not true. Out of anger, I told him that I had been taking care of the children alone and with little or no help from the family, had not even thought about taking anything from anyone or doing anything illegal. He was told that I was tired and to get money to put the children in this house I was prepared to do anything necessary, including hitting someone in the head. The next morning, he called me and said that he would loan me the money. On December 19, 1966, I closed on the house, we moved into the lower flat. We had a home for Christmas.

In the spring of 1967, I repaid my father the $300. The children were now in a home. I had placed them in school within walking distance of the house. The 2nd floor flat had been rented to a young couple that had one young son. They were helpful in watching out for the children when I was not home. Through our many experiences of having to make do, the children now 9, 8 and 6 were very responsible and helpful. They all had chores and duties that they performed to keep the house in order.

Greyhound had finished a successful operation at the New York World's Fair, where they had provided the ground transportation. They had removed musical horns from the vehicles that played a tune to their slogan: "Go Greyhound and Leave the Driving to Us". I had the maintenance Department put one of the horns on my company car. It was a real novelty for sales' purposes and when I arrived home, I could play it and my kids would hear it and know that I was home.

In the summer of 1967, Mrs. Frieda Schwartz, the children's grandmother came back to the country to visit the grandchildren and to see her daughter. We now had a nice place for her, where she could have her own bedroom. I had always had a great relationship with her, beginning with our first meeting in Berlin, when Vera took me home to meet the family. She was a very kind and loving person, who loved the children and was able to fill some of the void left by their mother. She spoke German to the children, very little English, which caused me to recall more of the German language that I had forgotten. Things were going smoothly until April when we received word that Mr. Schwartz, the children's grandfather, had been killed in a work-related accident. I located Vera and informed her of his death. I started to arrange for Mrs. Schwartz to return to Berlin, thinking that Vera was going home with her. Vera said that she couldn't go back with her mother, although I insisted that her mother needed her during this long, difficult trip back to Berlin and the services for her father. Vera remained in New York and didn't attend the services. Following the burial of Mr. Schwartz, we maintained close telephone and mail contact with the grandmother who was now alone.

We were in constant contact with Oma ("grandmother" in German) Schwartz in Berlin, who was now alone and missing her only grandchildren. She asked me in her letters and telephone calls if I would let the children come to Berlin and stay with her for a while. My mother was also living alone following her divorce from my father and had never traveled out of the country. I thought that this would be an opportunity for the children to experience life in another country. They would learn about their German heritage, the language, and spend more time with the grandmother that they loved and that loved them very much. When I offered my mother a chance to accompany them, she was excited. My Charter Commission agent was also a travel agent and the arrangements were made. On September 16, 1967, I took my mother and the children to New York, we visited Vera, their mother, that evening before they left, and on the following day they flew to Berlin, Germany, to be with Mrs. Schwartz. The children were enrolled in school in Berlin and the two grandmothers used the time to become more familiar with each other. Mother returned to Detroit after about three weeks in Berlin. I suggested that my mother visit some other cities in Europe, maybe Paris or London on her way home, but she chose not to, because she was traveling alone and was not an experienced traveler.

Most of the contact with the children and their grandmother was by mail and audio tapes, some of which I still have. They always said that they missed me, but that they were having a good time with their German relatives. The children were also using the opportunity to speak and write German. Denise, the oldest of the children, became very fluent in spoken and written German and used these skills in employment and social activities as an adult. We exchanged pictures, correspondence, tapes and occasionally a telephone call to stay in touch.

On or about February 1968, I received a letter announcing The Annual Marketing Meeting for Eastern Greyhound Lines in Richmond, Virginia, on March 5 and 6th. I was advised that they were going to highlight some of the successes of the Detroit, Michigan marketing program. The company usually placed two ranking supervisors in an assigned room. I was not surprised that in 1968, I had a single room. I was surprised at what followed.

The host hotel was the John Marshall. No reply was required; all Marketing Managers and supervisors were required to attend. My assistant and I arrived on the afternoon of March 4th via Greyhound. We were told that a "Hospitality Reception" was being held in room 1226. We attended the reception and exchanged greetings with the other supervisors, managers and officials. Following the reception, my assistant, the Terminal Manager from Indianapolis, and others joined me in my room. Prior to going to dinner, someone showed me a card entitled, "Thirty-Two Hundred Club", with a portion left blank marked "Admit My Guest" -- Resident Member Long. I was told that they were given out at the hospitality suite. The group went to dinner and enjoyed each other's company. On Tuesday the first day of the meeting, the theme was "Greyhound: The Company Who Cares."

The meeting was very informative, and we were again told that Greyhound was an "Equal Opportunity Employer" and the importance of the Special Market activities was explained in great detail. On Tuesday evening, Greyhound hosted another reception in the Colony Room of the John Marshall hotel. The Director of Passenger Sales and Service was at the door and had a box of book matches in his hand. He didn't give or offer one to my assistant or me; he simply said, "I know you people, go on in." Following the reception, a group of attendees, both white and Negro, were talking, and someone said that there was a reception for Greyhound attendees at the Holiday Inn.

We took cabs to the motel and upon entering the motel, the Director of Customer Sales and Services and The Director of Package Express intercepted us. They said that they needed to talk to the Negro members of the group. They tried to explain that this was a restricted club and that they did not admit Negroes. There was a very hot discussion with me speaking for the others. I questioned who they were trying to protect and why. I told them that, under no conditions, would I allow a company or employer to invite me to anything and discriminate against me. I told them that I was returning to Detroit that evening and resigning. The other two Negroes, who were City Marketing Representatives, tried to persuade me to stay. I returned to my hotel room, packed and left Richmond on the next bus.

When I arrived home the next morning my telephone began to ring. It started with my supervisor and friend Joe McCue to whom I explained what happened in Richmond and my resignation had nothing to do with him or our relationship. Over the course of the day, calls that I received included: a) the Vice President of Special Markets and the Greyhound Corporation, (who had been one of four Negro Greyhound employees at the meeting), b) the Vice President of Marketing of the Eastern Greyhound Lines, and c) the President of Eastern Greyhound Lines. Each person apologized on behalf of Greyhound and they asked me to withdraw my resignation. I thanked each of them and told them 'no thanks'.

Later, the President of Eastern Greyhound Lines called me again and asked that I go to my office and pick up the company car and come to Cleveland to talk with him. I agreed and we had a long talk, during which he apologized many times. At the end of our talk he said, "I am glad that we worked this out and that you are returning to work." I replied that we had not reached any agreement and that I needed to know where he wanted me to park the company car. He asked me to return it to Detroit, which I did. I had so much to lose, as the children were still in Berlin and I had to purchase tickets for their return, make the side note and payment on the house that I had bought and protect whatever security I had made for our family of four. Yet, I still had to be true to myself, while making a stand for future Negroes that would come this way.

The next day, I received a call from the President of the Greyhound Corporation. He identified himself and asked if I would talk to Mr. Gerald Trautman, Chairman of the Board. I agreed to speak with him. He began by telling me that he was aware of what had happened in Richmond and asked me to accept his apology on behalf of The Greyhound Corporation. He said that he was aware of my performance in Detroit and that the company wanted me to reconsider. He further said that if I would, he would give me his personal assurance that nothing like this would ever happen again within the Greyhound Corporation. I had met Mr. Trautman before. He was the Chairman of The Board; he could ensure that this never happened again, and more importantly, I believed him to be a man of his word. Many people who knew the risk that I was taking said that the company just wanted to get past this incident and that they would terminate me at the first chance that they got. I didn't intend to give them a chance; I agreed to return to work. The risk I took was worth it. The commitment was from the top, and no such incidents ever reoccurred within Greyhound (of which I was aware) and I remained employed by Greyhound until 1983.

In the summer of 1968, I was unable to get a response from the children and or the grandmother. After trying many times around June and not receiving a response from the grandmother or the children, I enlisted the U.S. State Department to contact the grandmother. They reported that they had advised her of my concern, that she and the children were fine and that they would contact me. In July 1968, I arranged for the children to be sent back to New York via Pan American Airlines. When my brother Delano and I met them at the airport, the children were excited to see us, and they immediately told me that they had met some other children on the plane whose father knew me. When we located the other children and their parents, I was amazed that it was Captain Gardner (The first and only roommate in the flat when I first arrived in Berlin).

CHAPTER 13

TRANSFERRING TO THE CHICAGO CORPORATION OFFICE

In November 1968, the Vice President of Special Markets for Greyhound Corporation contacted me and offered me a promotion to Director, Special Markets. It would require that I transfer to the Corporation office in Chicago, Illinois. I took the offer and on December 1, 1968, I became the Director, Special Marketing, and the Greyhound Corporation. My first assignment was to meet him in Miami, Florida, for activities surrounding the Orange Blossom Classic. The travel by air and the extent of expenses allowed were a welcome change from Greyhound requirements that you travel by bus or company car and stay at less expensive hotels. We had reservations at one of the finest hotels along Miami Beach, dined at the finest restaurants and moved via cab or limo. We attended affairs and activities that were restricted to an elite group of executives and dignitaries.

This first assignment was fun and exciting. I looked forward to the future in this position. We returned to Chicago, Illinois, and I moved into a new office in the Greyhound Corporate Headquarters.

I knew many of the people that were working with me from my experiences with Greyhound and I met the others in a short period. Unfortunately, the increase in salary was neither enough to relocate my family and hire a housekeeper in Chicago, nor was it initially enough for me to add a second home for myself in Chicago. It was as though I was back to 1962, only now, back to the Y.M.C.A. in downtown Chicago. Trying to hold down expenses, I asked for the cheapest room that they had. The desk clerk told me that I wouldn't be able to manage it, but I insisted. When I unlocked the door, I found that there wasn't enough room for my two suitcases and me to be in the room, with the bunk bed down at the same time. I returned to the desk and took the larger room, about 4 feet larger and with the bathroom down the hall. I would check into and out of the YMCA as I traveled around the country and between Detroit and Chicago. I even tried living with an aunt of mine that was by herself; however, she wouldn't give me a key and I had to leave the house at 5:00 AM when she did and remain out until she was home. This was too much like my early 1962 days in Cleveland, sleeping on the Elevated Train, the station benches and being the first one at the office. Unable to handle this arrangement, I thanked her and rented a cheap, small-furnished apartment on the North side of Chicago in a less than desirable location. It reminded me of my room on 69th Street in Cleveland in 1962, lots of police activity around the entrance on a regular basis. A couple of pots, a couple of dishes, basic utensils and I was back in business. I had a place to stay when

I was in Chicago; I was now traveling around the country, using an expense account to offset some of the additional costs. I returned home each weekend, which made life fast but acceptable.

The position of Director Special Markets was a newly created position. Before my arrival in Chicago, Grey Advertising worked with The Vice President of Special Markets, setting appointments for his appearances on local and national media outlets. In addition to scheduling his media appearances, they also organized public service activities where Greyhound would honor minorities in cities that we were scheduled to visit and invite local citizens to attend luncheons or dinners. I assumed the responsibility for arranging these activities, both by using many of my established contacts and by creating new ones.

Unlike Grey Advertising, I was subordinate to my new supervisor and found him difficult to work with. On many occasions, I would find it impossible to get him to arrive at the activity on time. I found myself apologizing for his improper behavior when I could not correct his action or activity. He thought it was necessary to remind me about what was proper behavior in dealing with females around the office, although I was single and had never given anyone reason to suggest that I had spoken or acted improperly. There were only three Negroes in the corporate office at the time: V.P. Special Markets, Yvette, a female secretary and me. I was very aware of proper protocol and of the situation that had occurred in Richmond, Virginia, in March of 1968.

Here I was, interacting on a daily basis with the same corporate officers that I had challenged about their proper conduct 12 months ago. In order to try and rebuild the relationships, I kept a candy jar on my desk with Peanut Brittle in it. I thought it was a nice way of being friendly and many of the executives, managers and clerical employees would stop by and visit while they picked up some candy.

One morning The President of The Greyhound Corporation came into my office. This was not strange because he stopped in often. He asked where my supervisor was, and since he was out of town, I had his itinerary. I told him the city that he was in and offered to contact him. He said, "Fred, we have a problem. Your secretary (naming her) came to me and told me that she was pregnant by him and that he won't do anything for her." I had experienced many bad times in my life, but never had I felt so hurt and ashamed. My supervisor had admonished me many times not to make any advances towards her or any other female in the office. She was married and I had never given her any thought. I had done nothing. I was so very ashamed for my position, myself, my company and especially for my supervisor. The President left my office, after telling me that he would make the contact himself. I immediately called my supervisor and told him about my conversation with the President. "Did you cover for me?" he asked. "I didn't know anything about you and the secretary," I said. "Well, you could have covered for me," he responded. The secretary left the company and nothing else was said about it to me. There were other situations that I felt were inappropriate, which also made me ashamed and uncomfortable.

Near the end of July 1969, I decided that I needed to find other employment within the company or somewhere else. The position that I left in Detroit was filled and I didn't want to start over. I was on assignment in Cincinnati, Ohio, when I received a telephone call from the President of Greyhound Lines East who was also in the city. We met for lunch and he said that he had heard that I was upset with my present supervisor and considering leaving the company. I told him that this was true. He asked me if I would consider coming to Cleveland as a director and being on his staff. I assured him that I would be happy to make the change. On August 16, 1969, I was appointed Director of Tours, Greyhound Lines East with an office in Cleveland, Ohio. The children were in Detroit, Wilda was in Chicago, and I moved into a hotel in Cleveland.

The experience and success that I had in Detroit was valuable in my new assignment and I applied some of the procedures into the tour program throughout Greyhound Lines East. We expanded the tour program, wrote manuals, bulletins and directives to ensure that there was uniformity and quality in the tour program. Reports and reporting procedures were reviewed and adjusted to identify errors, ensure profitability, and to make improvements. The Vice-President of Marketing, Greyhound Lines East, his other staff members, and I visited and presented a marketing program, "Fast Start 70," in every major market within the division (every major city east of the Mississippi River).

On October 29, 1969, Wilda and I were married in Chicago, Illinois. I continued to make my weekend visits to Detroit to be with the children and my new wife. In December, we moved into a rented home in Shaker Heights, Ohio, and the five of us spent our first Christmas together. Wilda had worked as a secretary before we were married. She was agreeable to assisting me with the tour program after the normal office hours. The office had an IBM memory typewriter that my secretary couldn't operate but that Wilda could. We worked together evenings to rewrite the manuals, itineraries and tour outlines. Through the advertising agency, we developed additional points of sale materials and distributed it. I spent many days on the road visiting the Greyhound Travel Bureaus throughout the east and dealing with tour operators and vendors that were included in our programs. The new programs were successful.

While working as Director of Tours I met with the president of our division and he confided in me that the company was considering filing with the Interstate Commerce Commission for rights throughout the southern states where Trailways operated. He requested that I make a fact-finding trip to the area and report back to him. I had my secretary make reservations in Memphis, TN, Jackson, MS, Montgomery, AL and Baton Rouge, LA. She was instructed to make some of the reservations using my name and home address and others using my job title. I thought that this would be a great opportunity to determine how Negroes were being handled at some of the hotels that Greyhound had contracts with.

Things went well at most locations, with the notable exception of The Pick Hotel in Baton Rouge. When I registered, I was given a small room that appeared to be used for storage or maid quarters. I requested a change, upgrade, and was told that this was all that was available.

In Montgomery I walked in wearing casual clothing. I approached the desk where the young female clerk and a bellman were working. It appeared that I was a customer. I don't know if the fact that the name was "The Jefferson Davis Hotel" had anything to do with it. When I told her my name, she checked the files and asked me my name again. After another check, she asked if it could be under another name. The bellman was watching, listening, and wondering if I was in the wrong place. I told her that I did not use any other name and asked her, "Do you have a reservation for Mr. Frederick Bowman?" When she said yes, I said, "well that is me." She said "front" to the bellman that was close and listening. He came and took my bags, still suspicious of my being in the right place.

When we walked towards the elevator, he kept looking at me for some sign that I was uncomfortable. When the elevator arrived on the top floor, he looked at the key and got excited. "You are in the Presidential Suite, who are you?" I told him to unlock the door and we would talk. When inside I explained to him my position and that I controlled the purchase of many hotel rooms for Greyhound around the county. "Welcome to The Jefferson Davis. What can I do for you?" he answered. I had had a conversation with a young baggage agent at the Greyhound station prior to arriving at the hotel. I invited him to visit me at the hotel to discuss moving into supervision. I had the bellman shop for some drinks and refreshments, and he set everything up very nicely. The young Negro Baggage Agent was also impressed. We had dinner and discussed how to apply for and get into supervision. A few years later I met him again, and he was the city Sales Representative in Montgomery.

In April 1971, I met with the President of Greyhound Lines East to discuss the employment practices of the company. He expressed concern that there was no one of color in the Industrial Relations Department, where hiring and firing policy was established and enforced. He asked if I would consider making a move into the department. When the City Marketing Manager from Pittsburgh, PA, was brought in to replace me as Director of Tours, I was appointed Director of Industrial Relations effective April16, 1971. The territory was the same --everything east of the Mississippi River, south of Canada, and north of Key West, Florida. The department was responsible for employment and compensation policies, union contract negotiations, grievance hearings, arbitrations, and the company's equal employment enforcement and government contract compliance.

Most of the department's responsibilities were new to me and required that I accelerate my learning process and become knowledgeable of them quickly. Many hours were spent reading union contracts and company policy bulletins, as well as state and federal regulations dealing with employment. Not only was I more knowledgeable than Mr. George Green (Director of Industrial Relations & Personnel in former Eastern Greyhound Lines) about the policies that were in effect for his territory, but also more familiar with the policies that were in effect for the former Southern Greyhound Lines. Additionally, in 1971, there were pockets of resistance in the southern part of the company that were not too receptive to me and to the changes that were coming. I had visited many of the offices in the south as Director of Special Markets and/or Director of Tours, and met many of the managers and employees, making it a bit easier for me.

The fact was that I had been placed in the position by and with the support of the President also helped. The Vice President of Industrial Relations and Personnel was a senior manager, nearing retirement. A junior supervisor in the department that had been there for some time had strong knowledge of the contracts and policies. Relying on the success in my earlier Detroit experience, I depended on the department's other employees for information and assistance. I found everyone helpful and I developed rapidly into a knowledgeable Industrial Relations Director. Greyhound had always been lacking in the training of employees … and especially supervisors. With this new position, I found an opportunity to influence the company policy towards the establishment of training programs. I accepted the responsibility for developing and presenting new training programs, and in addition to my other responsibilities, made the inclusion of training more acceptable.

With assistance from another supervisor in the department, we developed training programs for supervisors to assist them with hiring, discipline, counseling, EEO policies and terminations. We took the programs to supervisors in the field and we brought then into the General office in Cleveland for training. In addition to the education that they received, it also allowed field supervisors to meet and establish a working relationship with staff members that had only been names and titles before their General Office training sessions.

CHAPTER 14

BECOMING INDUSTRIAL
RELATIONS DIRECTOR

On a training trip to New York City, the other supervisor named "Bob", who was making his first visit to the "Big Apple", accompanied me. He was in awe of the sights and sounds of the city, as we stood at a window of the Regional office on 8th Street on the mezzanine level, overlooking the activities on the street below. During early afternoon, you could observe the prostitutes offering their wares, pick-pockets doing their thing, and street people wandering among the city's residences where people were going about their normal activities, without concern. I pointed out a street person, just below us, going through a trash bin in search of lunch. Shortly after, Bob focused on the person going through the trash; the street person had found a half-eaten submarine sandwich. As we watched, he carefully took the meat from what was left of the sandwich, held it up and ate it, one piece at a time until he finished. The sight made Bob sick and he turned away. I called out to him to look back as the person reached back into the trash and took out a napkin and carefully dabbed his mouth clean. I then reminded Bob,

"Cleanliness was next to Godliness." During training classes, I told the story often, with Bob assuring non-believing students that it was true.

The Vice President of Industrial Relations and Personnel retired at the end of January 1974, and Mr. George Green was promoted to Vice President of Industrial Relations and Personnel, effective February 1, 1974; I became Director of Industrial Relations and Personnel for Greyhound Lines East. With more job titles came more responsibilities and a little more money. I became more involved in labor matters, contract negotiations, grievance hearings, arbitrations and the coordination of the implementation of the company's equal employment activities. I now had the ability to "police" those concerning potential violations of corporate policies. This was a difficult time, during which long held attitudes about race, gender, physical stature and appearance were being challenged through union grievances, local, state and federal Equal Employment Commissions and the courts.

I found myself traveling continuously around the division, meeting with company managers, employees, union representatives, agencies investigators, hearing officers and attorneys and/or in court. In addition to the travel requirements, I found myself in constant conflict with someone--an employee, a manager, some group, some agency, some law, and/or someone's belief. In other words, I was in a hostile environment most of the time. I was often thought to be too much of either a turncoat, a "house Negro", or too much of an advocate of company employees/applicants, failing to support management objectives, or too much anti-Civil Rights enforcement. Despite this, I was able to use my position to bring about many changes and improvements within the company.

On field trips, I also contacted employees and other persons that were not included in recruiting efforts in their city or area and encouraged them to apply for higher or better positions. I also advised them on ways to prepare for tests and interviews. On one occasion, I spoke with the secretary to the Director of Tours – a young Negro single mother, after the Director had left the position. I suggested that she consider applying for the position. Her response was nothing that I would put in this book, nor was it very respectful. Later she came to me, apologized, and explained that my suggestion was so unthinkable that she had spoken out of surprise that I would say something like that. She then asked me what made me think that she could get the job. I told her that she should go home that evening and write down all of the reasons that she should be considered for the job and that the first thing that she should put on her list was that she knew all of his correspondence, contact names and where the files were. She was to come back to me with her list and I would help her. When she returned with her list, I told her that I would help her prepare a resume and a cover letter. She suggested that we have dinner at her house and work there. I countered that we should work at my house and my wife would prepare dinner. I believe that you should "practice what you preach" and I was teaching proper conduct and respect.

I helped her to prepare the two items and had her rewrite the cover letter, since I knew that the Vice-President of Marketing, for whom I worked directly, might recognize my style and wording. I further explained that they probably would not make her a director, but she might initially be offered the assignment as a supervisor or manager. Within a week after the letter was sent, the Vice President of Marketing came to me and said that he had received a letter from her. He was impressed with her presentation, was considering an offer and wanted to know what I thought. I read the information and agreed that it was (with an internal smile) impressive. Within a week, she became the Supervisor of Tours, and years later became the manager of my Chicago office when I became Vice President of Charter Services.

We located and tested many minority and female applicants for supervisory and management positions throughout Greyhound Lines East. I often made a mental note of qualified applicants and supervisors that could be considered for promotion. In addition, I had the responsibility for preparing reports that were sent to the Federal government and meeting with reviewing compliance personnel. Many of the compliance efforts required that we had minority and female representation in all departments in the company. The Traffic Department was responsible for the company's route operating authority and application for new routes, which was an important department within the company and one that was the last to integrate. After several attempts to obtain their compliance, I provided them with the name of a young entry-level black supervisor in the Detroit terminal and insisted that he be considered. He was promoted into the department and, years later, he became the Vice President of the corporate department with that responsibility.

In July 1974, Greyhound Lines East had a total of one hundred-twenty minorities in decision making positions: 111 supervisors, 8 managers and 1 director. Included in these decision-making positions were 33 females (including 8 Negroes) in supervisory or management positions. During the driver hiring session in 1974, Greyhound Lines East hired 40.4 % minorities within a total of 779, of which 7 were females and 4 were white and 3 Negro. This may not be impressive to some, but in 1962, I was among the first Negro supervisors hired. During the same time-period (July 1974), Greyhound Lines West had a total of forty-eight minorities in decision-making positions: 45 supervisors, 2 managers, and 1 director. Two of the supervisors were female. The West hired 19.0% Negro drivers, yet hired no female drivers. I credit much of our success in the east to our President, Mr. James Kerrigan, who supported our efforts towards diversifying Greyhound.

The Operators contract expired on October 31, 1974, and we began our negotiations in Phoenix, Arizona, in August and obtained a contract settlement on November 24th. This was following much planning, caucuses, many meetings and a brief work stoppage. This was my first and only year on the national negotiations team. Mr. Vander Brown, Sr., Director of Industrial Relations for Greyhound Lines West, was also on the bargaining committee for the company. This was the first time that two Negroes had represented Greyhound Lines in national negotiations. Following the success of obtaining a new contract that covered all of the members in the country, we were taken to breakfast by the then President of Greyhound Lines Inc., at the Camelback Inn, Scottsdale, Arizona. He said that he had news for all of us that were on the bargaining committee, those who were assigned to the Industrial Relations Department in San Francisco and Cleveland. I was thinking bonus; instead he announced that he was moving the entire group to Phoenix, Arizona, into the Corporate Office in May of 1975.

CHAPTER 15

MOVING TO PHOENIX

On May 1, 1975, I was assigned to the position of Director of Employee Relations, Greyhound Lines Inc. with an office in Phoenix, Arizona. This was another separation from the family after we agreed that the children would not be taken out of school before the end of the semester. After a short hotel stay and without a car in Phoenix, I moved into a low budget studio apartment within walking distance of the office. I had visited Phoenix several times and worked there for periods of days, weeks and months; however, I had never had a residence there or visited anyone's home there. My expectation of Phoenix as a place to live and raise a family was low.

My new assignment represented a requirement that I travel to cities throughout the country and cover Greyhound facilities nationwide. I had the most experience in the areas of Equal Employment Opportunity, Contract Compliance, Affirmative Action, including the laws and the agencies that enforced them. Thus, I was assigned to handle all such cases for Greyhound Lines and some of the other companies within the Transportation Group. My travels and experiences were extensive as they included charges and complaints related to race, sex, color, nationality, ability and veteran's status from across the country. Complaints were received directly from employees, unions, as well as local, state and national agencies. My involvement included direct contact with applicants, employees, managers, government agencies, unions, organizations, community groups, lawyers and the courts. Many of these activities were conducted alone, in person and often in hostile surroundings. The four years that I spent in Cleveland in the Industrial Relations Department taught me what to expect and how to prepare.

By 1975, more people were aware of their rights and willing to challenge companies and organizations. Commissions and courts were ruling in favor of more complaints and awarding monetary settlements. The Women's Movement made females more aware of their rights and benefits due them. Most companies and many of the organizations were behind the curve on affirmative action and compliance. My assignment was to advise management of the law, rules and regulations, obtain our company compliance and to minimize the company's negative public EEO image and/or monetary exposure. If this appears to be a major assignment, it was that and more.

One of the major problems with dealing with discrimination of any nature is that both the accuser and the accused believe or profess to believe that they are correct. Most resolutions require adjustments, change, compensation and/or rejection of claim. In the process of handling most cases, neither side obtains total satisfaction. Yes, if you are responsible for handling a charge, complaint or lawsuit, someone is going to be mad at you for the way that it ends – regardless of how you dispose of it. Although I spent as much time as possible handling labor matters that were not EEO-related, most of my time was spent dealing with them.

I have been personally dealing with discrimination since I was old enough to understand that I was black and, to some people, that meant you were less and should be treated with less respect. I have been involved in ensuring that this not happen to me or anyone else, as long as I could do something about it.

My involvement with "Equal Opportunity" started in Saginaw, Michigan as a child who fought, if necessary, to obtain the respect of other kids. As a teenager in Detroit, Michigan, along with my older brothers, I was very active in the Detroit N.A.A.C.P. Youth Council. We spent many days and evenings in passive, nonviolent testing of the Michigan anti-discrimination laws concerning public accommodations. We were harassed and detained several times until the Detroit Police learned that the law was on our side. Over the years and before joining Greyhound, I had learned that it was much easier to bring about change from the inside than from the outside. On the outside, you can only try to know and understand what is going on, on the inside. To see what is going on, to know the people and have them know you and what you will and won't do, provides you an advantage in solving problems of any type. I also learned that much of the discrimination that exists in the world is the result of either the lack of or a limited personal contact, and social experiences with different people, as opposed to family, neighborhood, school, church or employment. I had the opportunity to make contact and interact with many different people from around the country and the world.

On one occasion, a vice-president friend in the company busted me when he said, "You think that you are getting away with something when you start to speak to people without addressing them by name." I was moving around the country, city-by-city and day-by-day -- no one could expect me to know the name of all of the people with whom I dealt. Realizing that I could improve my interactions, I decided to see how many names of people that I had contact with who I could remember. The results were amazing, in that when I spent enough time with people, I would learn something about them, their family, experience or background that would trigger my memory and remind me of their name.

I found that I could greet people by name and if I needed to remind myself of the names of people in a city where there was a company directory, I would brush up on the names of the personnel before I arrived. As a result, I knew many employees and people in many cities, not only by name, but also something about them. When I contacted then about something, I was able to get their assistance or cooperation because they knew me, and I knew them. It was very important that I had this type of cooperation because I was operating out of other cities and other offices much of the time and when I needed something from cities across the country, I could contact someone that would willingly assist me.

For example, the law department told me on Friday evening that we needed a personal file from Boston, Mass. for a court case on Monday. I called an employee by name, asked him to retrieve the file from a basement archive and express it to me. He willingly did what I asked. It arrived Monday morning and the lawyers were surprised that I had that type of contact. There were many interesting challenges during the eight years that I worked in the Industrial Relations Department, more than I can recount in this memoir, so I'll tell some that are the most memorable.

Greyhound was having a number of complaints in the Washington, D.C./Richmond, VA area, including discrimination charges and union grievances. I found myself working that area so often that contacts thought that I lived in the area. I would make the trip to Washington at the start of each week and return home to Phoenix for the weekend. There was an occasion when I received a request to meet with a group of minority employees in Washington, D.C. area to review complaints about discrimination and unfair treatment. I explained that I would meet and listen to them, take notes on our discussions, return to the company and recommend corrective action where needed, and then report back to the group.

The meeting was held at a hotel that was some distance from downtown, and when I arrived, I found a large group of employees. Some had an attorney and were very disruptive and asked me to leave. I attempted to accommodate the group and to hear all sides. The group with the attorney kept interrupting the meeting and making comments about what they were demanding to be done. Unable to determine how the numbers would come out, I asked that those wanting me to remain to be seated, while those that wanted me to end the meeting and leave to stand up. Following a quick headcount, I advised the group standing that they were outnumbered and that they were to leave. Unhappy and loud, they left. We had a good discussion that resulted in changes and improvements. When it was time for me to leave, I found myself alone and concerned about the angry group that I had excused. I requested the desk clerk to call a cab and had him pull up very close to the front entrance. I arrived back at my hotel without incident, but the following evening, the audiotapes from the meeting were taken (stolen) from my hotel room, leaving me only with my notes.

In another example, my office received a complaint from EEOC, alleging racial discrimination from a black driver. He had been terminated for failure to comply with the company's personal appearance policy, which did not permit beards. The driver and complainant ("Mr. Black") alleged that he suffered from hair bumps (folliculitis) and this would limit his ability to shave. I arranged for a meeting with him at the Greyhound DC terminal. "Mr. Black" arrived with his attorney and displayed a neatly trimmed full beard. I informed him that the company policy applied to everyone, male, female, black, white, yellow, etc. I asked him if he had pictures of himself with the beard, and if he didn't, would he allow me to take one. I then told him that if he would shave off the beard, it would not affect his charge that had already been filed and I would reinstate his employment that day. His attorney became outraged that I was giving his client advice and I reminded him that he was our employee first and his client second. I also reminded him that his attorney or EEO would not cover his lost wages during the process of the complaint. He took the advice from his attorney and EEOC and kept his beard. The company sustained "Mr. Black's" discharge in arbitration, and we won the litigation. He remained discharged.

During one series of complaints, we were using a prestigious law firm in Washington and another in Richmond. Being the company's representative, I worked very closely with the two firms. In Washington, they had provided me with a temporary office. The telephone was ringing on my desk one day and I didn't answer it because I thought that it was for someone in the firm. One of their staff came in and explained that this was my telephone that they had assigned to me.

Much of the time and effort in handling arbitration and court cases involves the review of the facts, identifying potential supporting witnesses and preparing them to present testimony. Before a witness is asked a question, the person or attorney should know what the answer will be. You need to have the next question ready or know how you are going to react if you do not receive the answer that is expected. Every witness that is prepared is told to give yes or no answers to questions, if possible, and not to volunteer any additional information.

After a long preparation session in Richmond, Virginia, one night the company attorney was questioning an Assistant Regional Manager concerning a discharge that was being arbitrated. Contrary to our instructions, he began to give a long, unsolicited answer to a question. Having been in this situation before and not being able to do anything about it, I now found myself close to the witness with a table between us. Without thinking, I kicked the witness in the leg and his voice went down like a recording that had the electricity turned off. It was so strange that everyone in the room was trying to figure out what happened. I too was shocked at what I had done, and at the same time, amused at everyone's reaction, while also trying to hold back my laugher. After a couple of minutes, the attorney asked another question and I couldn't hold back any longer – I broke out laughing. This really confused everyone, and I apologized for my outburst. During the automobile ride back to Washington, our attorney said that he couldn't understand what had happened to the witness's voice and what caused me to break out in laugher later. I explained that this was the first and only time that I had been able to react when our witness was about to kill our case, after which I couldn't believe that I had done it. Yes, we won the case.

Approximately one year after "Mr. Black" and I met in the DC terminal, I was returning to my Washington hotel after midnight from dinner, during which I had consumed a couple of cocktails. It was cold outside, and the city was torn up while they were building the subway system. When I was passing a construction site, I thought I heard someone calling, "Mr. Bowman!". Not seeing anyone around and the time of night made me a little concerned and I walked a little faster. I then saw a figure come up out of the below ground site and call, "Mr. Bowman," and move in my direction. I could not believe that someone working on a construction site would recognize me in the dark. Who would want to talk to me this time of the morning? The man in the work clothes said, "Mr. Bowman, you probably don't remember me, but my name is "Mr. Black" and I was a driver for Greyhound before I was terminated for having a beard." I looked at him and said, "Yes I do, "Mr. Black"... I remember well." He then explained that he had lost his wife, family, and house. He wished that he had listened to me and followed my advice. He asked me if there was anything that I could do to help him regain employment with Greyhound.

I explained that I didn't conduct business on the street, late at night and after having a drink. He was instructed to call me the next day at the Washington, D.C. Greyhound terminal, which he did. I told him that there probably wouldn't be anything that I could do, but I would try and get back to him. I checked his past personnel file and found that he had been a satisfactory employee before growing the beard. Being tired from the many trips to the Washington area and desiring to break the backlog of complaints and problems in the area, I proposed to the company and the Amalgamated Transit Union that we give "Mr. Black" a driver-refresher course, and following satisfactory completion, we rehire him with seniority ahead of the soon-to-graduate driver's class. After several meetings with all concerned, my proposal was accepted, and he was returned to work. Eventually, employee relations in Washington, DC, improved and I made fewer trips to the area.

Similarly, a black driver in Philadelphia filed a discrimination complaint, alleging that the company policy of no beards was discriminating against Negroes. The EEOC processed the case and this case was heard in the Federal District Court in Philadelphia. Following testimony, the Federal Judge ruled in favor of the plaintiff. Knowing that the judge had misinterpreted the law, I insisted that our Law Department appeal the ruling. The Federal Court of Appeals overturned the case.

Another example was where my office telephone was ringing when I arrived one morning. The voice on the line was crying and screaming so loud that I couldn't understand what she was saying. I said, "I can't understand you. Please calm down". Still crying she said, "You people are killing my father, you're killing my father." I had no idea what she was talking about and asked her to calm down and try to explain what she was talking about. She said that her father had worked for Greyhound in the Indianapolis, IN, terminal for almost twenty years, most recently as a supervisor. She explained that Greyhound had accused him of theft when he sent an item with a baggage tag and didn't travel with it, instead of shipping it by Greyhound Baggage Express, and he had been terminated. Her father was at home suffering from what she thought was a heart attack and wouldn't go to the hospital because he had no insurance and was afraid that it would wipe out the family savings. I had no knowledge of this incident and told her that I would check and determine what, if anything, I could do and call her back. I told my manager, Vice President of Industrial Relations, about the telephone call and that I was checking on the facts.

When I talked to the Regional Vice President responsible for the area, he confirmed that the termination had taken place and for the reason that she had related. I questioned if he thought that the penalty was too severe, which he didn't. This information was passed on to my manager who said that I should leave it alone. When considering the violation, the years of service and lack of representation to present his case, I didn't feel that the employee was getting fair treatment. In response to my manager's question as to what should be done; I said that someone should appeal it to a higher level. Since he was that level and not willing to assist, it meant appealing it to the President. Although he didn't think that it was a good idea, he said if I felt that strongly about it, I could try.

The President refused to consider any relief, although I told him that I was handling union (contract employee) cases across the country where the violation was handled with less than discharge, less than 30 days suspension. He said that it was theft, he would not consider intervening. My manager questioned if I was now satisfied and was surprised when I said no, everyone reports to someone. "You are not talking about going over his head, are you?" he asked. "Not if you direct me not to," I replied. "It's your call and you will have to live with it," he said. I then called the office of the Vice Chairman of transportation in the Greyhound Corporation and requested a meeting.

I met and explained the telephone call from the daughter, the facts that I had obtained from my investigation, and asked him if he thought we had treated the employee fairly. "No, go tell the President – no, I'll tell the President – you go tell your manager to reinstate him, restore his benefits and call the daughter, tell her to take her father to the hospital." I did and I slept well that night. The employee was hospitalized, and he made his transition about a week later.

I was in court in Cincinnati, Ohio, handling a lawsuit when I received a call from the President advising me that a group of minority employees in New Orleans, LA, were requesting I meet with them to review their complaints and grievances. I explained that I was trying to finish this court case but that I was sick with the flu. I requested that the company send someone else so that I could return to Phoenix and see my doctor. He thought that it was important that I go and said that he would arrange for me to see a doctor in Cincinnati. After a doctor visit and receiving some medication, I booked a flight to New Orleans that evening. I asked that the local personnel send me the personnel files of some of the employees that were requesting the meeting, so that I could be knowledgeable of the people that I was to meet with. I scheduled a meeting for the next evening and read files late into the night. Early the next morning, I was wakened by a call from the local manager asking if I had a radio in my hotel room. He told me that a group of employees were on the radio talking about the scheduled meeting and what was going to transpire. I tuned in and was surprised that they had plans for me that included presenting a list of demands. They did not intend to allow me to leave until they got what they wanted.

Following a conference call with the President and the legal department, I went to the radio station and requested a copy of the broadcast. They refused, until I reminded them that Greyhound was a major client, after which I received a copy. My travel equipment always included a tape recorder and a camera. I played the tape in another conference call for the company officers and the legal department in Phoenix. I explained that I was canceling the meeting because I refused to meet under these conditions or to be "held captive." I returned to the radio station, requesting and receiving time to make a rebuttal statement to explain why I would not meet with them that evening. I boarded a flight and returned to Phoenix.

Arriving in Phoenix, I was met with a message that there had been large numbers of minority drivers calling in sick and some schedules had to be cancelled. I went directly to my office where I met with company officers and we arranged to have drivers sent from locations across the country to restore the service before midnight. We sent certified letters to each driver demanding that they return to work or face termination. I called my wife and asked her to pack me another suitcase, reassuring her that I would be okay. I boarded another flight and returned to New Orleans before midnight. I stayed in New Orleans until I was sure that our operation was back on track. Those operators that refused to return were terminated. The company received discrimination complaints and grievances because of the action taken.

I scheduled and held several employee meetings in New Orleans, accompanied by two or more company officers. There were changes made as the result of those meetings that were proper and needed. It was years later, when we finished handling the union grievances and court cases that resulted from the action, yet the company was not found to have violated the contract or the law in the handling of this matter.

In another example, a file arrived in my office from California, outlining the termination of a terminal employee in Sacramento that had not been forwarded or handled properly. When I read the file, I was appalled that I had not been contacted before and that I believed that there was a substantial amount of liability involved. The employee, who was a ticket agent, had not performed satisfactorily, but had been allowed to retain employment. One evening, he had been drinking and had an accident. He was injured and his wife had been killed. After he returned to work and within a short period of time, he had another accident, which resulted in him becoming a paraplegic. Following hospitalization and rehabilitation, he attempted to return to work, yet the local manager refused to reinstate him.

The State of California provided him with additional training, offered to provide any special equipment that he needed, and contacted the local manager, who still refused to reinstate him. Years later, with a notice of a public hearing, a legal action caused them to return the employee to work and then to send me the file for handling. I was disappointed that our managers had not understood the laws and rights of handicapped persons. I explained that, in my opinion, the company was liable for lost wages during the years that we had not reinstated him. Furthermore, the company had failed to require any additional action, tests or physicals, before reinstating him. I advised my manager that I would attend the hearing without legal counsel, because any attorney would know that we were wrong. I thought that my experience would allow me to present the company's case, while not appearing to embarrass myself, due to proper legal presentation. The hearing lasted for two days and there was evidence from experts who deemed the employee fit for work, several times before the reinstatement.

Sometimes in hearings and court cases, you make arguments that are not reasonable or that you don't quite believe in. This was one of those cases and I did my job well. In order to do some of the things that I found myself doing, it required that I believe that the opposition had training, counsel and resources at their disposal as did the company. In other words, it's a fair fight if you don't cross the line and do something unethical. The local managers were impressed by my knowledge of the laws and my presentation. I expressed my disappointment with their handling of the case, and we reviewed the company policy and the laws. I told my manager and the local personnel that I expected them to find us liable and order restitution. Months later I received a large envelope from The California Civil Rights Commission, and they agreed with my position and found that the company owed him nothing. It was not what I wanted or expected. I was in shock, as I couldn't believe that they had come to that decision. Somebody or some persons let the employee down.

Greyhound had an agency that provided internal security in terminals, aboard buses and around other facilities. When they placed undercover agents at locations as employees, they occasionally found violations of company policy, including theft. On one occasion a group of employees in the Washington, D.C. and Philadelphia, PA area were found to be involved in the theft of tickets through their resale and misuse. Employees were interviewed and presented with evidence, including video and pictures. In all incidences, the employees, both terminal and drivers, resigned when faced with possible prosecution; however, there was one driver from

Philadelphia that refused to resign and the ATU {Amalgamated Transit Union) chose to take the case to arbitration.

Along with a Corporate Labor Attorney and many company witnesses that had been subpoenaed, I found myself locked in an expensive and lengthy arbitration. Some of the witnesses were undercover agents from the security unit. We had placed security guards on the entrances to the floors of the hotels where the witnesses were staying. Following the first day of the hearing, during which the union attorney raised several motions that had to be resolved before testimony could start, I realized that we were in a situation where it was going to be costly, time consuming, and that there was the possibility of our not prevailing. I also understood that if we did not win, and future cases where we presented employees with the option of resigning, they would be more likely to take their chance in arbitration. I needed to have the resignation of that last employee and have it quickly. I scheduled a meeting with the union attorney and discussed a possible solution. We agreed that he would resign and that the company would pay him a couple of thousand dollars.

I released the company witness and they returned to their duties, including the corporate attorney who had been with the company for over twenty years. The next day I was in another city handing another matter when I received a call from the company attorney who was very excited and wanted to know what my relationship was with the Vice Chairman of Transportation for the Greyhound

Corporation. I told him that I had known him for several years and that we had an understanding. Why was he asking? He said, "The Vice Chairman called me into his office this morning and told me I heard about the settlement in Philadelphia--we don't pay thieves and you are fired." He said that as he was leaving the office, he asked him who the company Industrial Relations person was that handled the case. He told him "Fred Bowman." The Vice Chairman said, "Oh, Fred was there and did it - you can go back to work." I was in the department and the company for years, following this incident, and The Vice Chairman never spoke to me about this case.

In another instance, I received a grievance from the Machinist Union in Chicago, IL, alleging disparity in treatment in the company reclamation plant. I spoke with the location management and their explanation did not provide a satisfactory explanation for the disparity in progression among employees in the apprentice program. It appeared that some individuals had been singled out for progression, while others were denied upgrades. After explaining that I could not justify their position, I scheduled a grievance hearing in Chicago. The union brought several very angry members and about three managers accompanied me. The discussion was extremely hostile and after a couple of hours, I believed that it was not improving. In an effort to change directions and believing that the reaction would be very hostile and angry, I proposed the following: "I propose that I be allowed to reduce all of the personnel in the program to the base rate of pay, retroactive by

30 days, after which I will review all persons in the program and place them in their rightful place and pay bracket." Since the reduction in pay was up to $3 dollars an hour for 160 hours, some people would not get a check the next payday and would owe the company money. I awaited the explosive reaction. To my surprise, the International Representative for the Union said, "That sounds fair to me." Trying not to display my surprise, I asked if he understood what I said, and I repeated it. He again agreed to the proposal. I asked for an adjournment so that I could have an agreement written up for us to sign, expecting someone to object before I came back with it.

The company manager asked me what I had done when we were back in our offices and I asked him what he thought I had proposed. He said that he thought I was taking money away from some employee and couldn't understand how the union was agreeing. I explained that he was right. I threw that out to try and let them vent their rage and then I was going to correct the problem, but they had accepted the proposal and I offered – in writing. When we resumed the meeting I read the proposal to the group once and then a second time. The International Representative said it was fine and we both signed it. When my manager read it, he responded: "Fred, I've been in this business over twenty years and I have never been able to take money away from the union. How did you do this?" Very carefully, I laughingly explained and then I went through the scenario of how it came about. We both knew that the union rep had erred in agreeing to this and that I would be hearing from them soon.

The next call that I received was from an angry Vice President of Maintenance who had heard that I had done something different during the hearing without his agreement. He hadn't read his copy yet assumed that I had given the union an advantage. I interrupted him and asked if he had read the agreement. When he continued to chastise me, I again told him to stop and read his copy. He said, "Damn, how did you get them to agree to that?" I explained to him as I had to my manager. He said "Oh… Goodbye". The next day I received a call from the International Representative who sounded like he was calling from underground. He said that he didn't understand the agreement, that the. employees were angry with him, and they were about to run him out of town. I explained what happened. I told him that I had repeated the agreement twice, read it twice and expected someone to object. He asked if I would immediately return the money to the employees that had lost wages and correct the conditions. He further agreed to some conditions, if I would comply, and I contacted the payroll department and had them issue checks. We didn't receive another grievance from that union about the reclamation plant before I left the department.

Early in my industrial relations assignment and while working in Cleveland, I accompanied a senior department manager into a southern city for contract negotiations with the union that represented mechanics in the south. I was new in the department and was there to learn, take notes, and assist. During the negotiations, the company representative proposed that we correct the provisions in the contract that he believed to be illegal because of racial discrimination. The company made several attempts to have the articles changed, after which the spokesperson from the union said: "we will change it when a Federal Judge makes us." I was extremely offended by his remarks and remembered them.

Years later, while working in Phoenix, I was assigned to handle a series of complaints from Negro maintenance employees, alleging racial discrimination by the company and the unions in the former Southern Greyhound Lines. The Miami, FL office of EEOC (Equal Employee Opportunity Commission) was handling the matter as a class action. After several meetings, where the progress was not what was desired by the commission, they sent the matter to their legal department. I realized that there was little chance to prevail, and that the liability was substantial. Therefore, I recommended to the company and the three unions involved, that they allow me to attempt to negotiate a less costly agreement. The conciliation manager in Miami, whom I had been working with, was unhappy with me for not agreeing to his terms. He said that the matter was now in the law department and they would not return it to conciliation. Following several discussions, based upon not only my challenging his ability to get the case returned to him, but also the fact that his department would not get the credit for any settlement, we met and agreed to a very reasonable financial settlement. The provisions in the contract had already been changed. The three unions and the company agreed to divide the financial settlement equally between the four defendant originations. When I contacted the unions to schedule an agreement-signing meeting, I was told that they had changed their minds and weren't going to pay anything.

I was very upset because I had worked long and hard to bring this matter to a reasonable solution and the EEOC representative was even more upset and was ready to take the matter back to the legal department for litigation. With the company approval, I assured the conciliation manager that Greyhound would assume responsibility for the full amount of the agreement, if the terms were allowed to stand, and we would only litigate the liability among the defendant organizations. It was agreed upon and the matter remained on hold until later. When I was on an assignment in the Northeast, I received an urgent call that I needed to be in Miami the next morning for the court case on this matter. I boarded the red-eye for Miami, arriving early that morning and checking into my hotel. I met with the company lawyers and went to Federal District Court. The company manager that had been at the union contract negotiations years earlier was sick and couldn't travel. I was one of the first witnesses called to the stand and spent most of the morning hours on the stand. I explained to the court the provisions of the contract, the efforts by the company to change them earlier, the union's response about the federal judge making them change, the negotiations, and the activity leading up to our being in court. The judge said that he was going to call a recess for lunch. He further said that he was duty-bound to take all of the testimony that was presented, to listen to all arguments and positions, but following my testimony he understood everything that he needed to know about the case. He then turned to a union lawyer and told him that they had a problem, after which he told the other union lawyers the same thing.

I advised our lawyers that I was going to my hotel for a quick nap and that they should call me when the union lawyers contacted them. I returned to the courthouse following the call from our lawyer and found the union representatives agreeable to accept the equal division that they had turned down. I reminded them that all offers that are rejected were off the table and I didn't know what they were proposing. My counteroffer was more than generous, in light of the additional work that they had caused me. The offer was for the company to donate less than 20% of the total and they could divide the remainder among themselves. Before they expressed too much dissatisfaction, I reminded them of the judge's comments and offered to go back into court to let him decide. Following the judge's agreement to seal the case, I believe that this was one of the few times that the union paid more than a company, in such a case.

There were many, many more interesting labor-related cases and activities, too many to include! I spent eight years in the Industrial Relation Department, during which I was involved in many confrontational situations, both within and outside of the company, in an effort to perform my assignment and bring about change and improvement. I made several requests to be reassigned to a position that required less time away from my family and one that was less adversarial. The only other person of color in the company at our level of Director was Vander Brown, Director of Personnel. We had put our careers on the line too many times as we sought policy changes and opportunities for minorities and females. In late 1979, the only Negro officer within Greyhound was the Vice President of Special Markets and The Greyhound Corporation, who never had more than six people in the company report directly to him.

CHAPTER 16

A CHANGE WAS COMING

The company had created a new department, Greyhound Group Travel, prior to my leaving the Industrial Relation Department. They brought in a female Vice President from outside the company to head it. The department consolidated Greyhound Highway Tours, the Greyhound Charter Service offices, some formally Loyal Travel offices, the International Sales Operation and the Charter Bus Control section. They recruited many young, attractive (mostly) white females with a college education. There were a small number of males that were from within the company, of which at least three were directors, and none were minorities. The Phoenix operation of the department was non-union. There were offices in major cities, such as Atlanta, Cleveland, Chicago and New York City, where each had a charter processing section. The headquarters' office was located in Phoenix, in a separate building next door to the Greyhound Tower. The department was given a great deal of support, electric/ technical equipment, autonomy, and independence from the parent company, Greyhound Lines Inc. For those who questioned the operation, their policies or procedures, they received rebuke and/or admonishment. I found some of their policies and procedures questionable, but it was a department that everyone knew to leave alone, including me.

One Saturday morning, I went to my office to leave files from my work and dictation from the week's travel and to pick up new files for my trip to Miami, Florida, the following Monday. The office was closed to the public and required that you show identification and sign in. When I signed the roster, I noticed that several senior officers and the Corporate Chairman were in the building. I also made a note of those officers that were not there, and I sensed a major purge within the company. The Vice-President of Industrial Relations called me on Monday morning before I boarded the plane and instructed me to call him as soon as I arrived in Miami. When I made the call from Miami, he began to tell me that there had been some changes in the company, when I stopped him and told him who I thought was gone and who was still there, based on what I had observed from the Saturday sign-in roster. The Vice-Chairman of Transportation, the President of Greyhound Lines Inc. and several Vice Presidents had been released.

In 1979 Greyhound Line Inc. brought in a Senior Vice President of Marketing from outside of the organization. I was out of town on assignment, when I heard that he was reorganizing the marketing department and seeking experienced personnel. I contacted him by telephone and arranged for an interview at his home that weekend when I would be in town. The interview went well; I received a job offer and accepted the position of Western Area Marketing Manager, with less title and a smaller area of territory in which to travel, but more money and less stress. I then contacted my manager and informed him that I was accepting a new assignment. The assignment lasted only six months but made me responsible for the development of a marketing plan, advertising and sales in the 14 western states for the company. I was in a position to develop and implement schedule changes and service improvements to increase sales and profits for the company.

In February 1980 I was contacted and offered the position of Vice-President of Group Travel. My first reaction was to reject the offer, although I had worked for eighteen years with an objective to becoming a Vice-President or higher. I knew that the person that replaced the already removed Vice-President had the responsibility for changing the training, efficiency, profitability and the poor reputation of the department. I had worked hard to establish a good professional reputation in the company and with persons that I had contact with outside. I didn't want to be associated with Group Travel. I was told that my background and reputation made me the best candidate for the assignment. With the understanding that I could change the name of the department to Greyhound Charter Services, I accepted. When I went over to the offices in Phoenix, I found that there were supervisors and managers sitting all over the place, even in the hallway. The Vice-President's office was beautifully furnished, had a large conference table and was larger than that of some corporate officers' offices. When I called the first meeting of my new staff, I requested that each person tell me what another person that I called by name had responsibility for and what their duties were. I found out quickly that much of the problems within the department was that they didn't know what the other managers did. We had a long session, during which the managers explained their duties. We began to develop some plans for training and written policies for the department that would bring about more interaction with other departments in the company.

My next action was to contact the Vice-President of Architectural Engineering and Property to discuss finding space for more offices for the managers. When I suggested that we use some of the space in my office, he measured it and said that we could not build the number of offices and still have the required space needed for the minimum size of a Vice-President's office. He was requested to make the changes, as I was not concerned about the size of my office and I wanted the managers to have proper office space. He replied that he never thought that he would ever hear a Vice-President say that he didn't care about having the minimum size office available to him. This was one of the first changes that we made. The department was instructed that we were selling charter "motor coach" service.

We were no longer in the bus business. We set up a large jar and every time someone used the word "bus" they had to put a quarter in the jar, which was to be used for a department function. I identified an employee in the department that had experience in training and created a training program. They proudly showed me the department's Quantel computer. Ours was the only department to have its own computer; I discovered that it was being used as a large typewriter. Each of the processing clerks in the main office had a desktop CRT (Cathode Ray Tube) color display monitor and a keyboard that sent charter information to the computer and allowed it to be printed out each evening. When the charter orders were printed each evening, several people would spend hours routing, packaging and overnight shipping to Greyhound dispatch offices throughout the country for processing and distribution to motor coach operators. There were few, if any, reports or records the computer maintained that could be used for analysis or marketing purposes.

When I approached the department responsible for computer programming about developing software programs that would make the computer useful and effective, I was told that my department was so low on the priority list that the equipment would be outdated before they got around to us. I met with my Administrative Director, who I felt was capable and inquired if he was interested in learning how to write computer programs. When he agreed, I contacted Quantel in California and arranged for him to be enrolled in their next class. When he completed the several weeks of courses and returned, I had him seek out a second person, a young, minority, military veteran and he was sent to California to complete the class.

I then met with the two of them and outlined what I visualized the department to be operating like, with the computer being properly utilized. Before I left the department in 1983, we had closed the other processing offices in other cities around the country, established digital telephone lines between the main office and all other offices in the country, established sufficient toll-free lines into the main office to handle all calls from around the country and from overseas. The digital lines (which were leased and dedicated) allowed us to transmit all data that was recorded at each office directly into the computer in Phoenix (a network).

My staff and I had immediate access to all charter information that Greyhound processed. We developed reports, comparisons, sales programs and marketing strategies that were meaningful. Although we were told that it couldn't be done, we developed programs and procedures that each evening allowed us to process, sort, and transmit charter orders directly to all Greyhound dispatch offices that had a teletype machine at no additional cost. To correct the procedures that had resulted in over a million dollars being misplaced or uncollected revenue, we established requirements that a $50 per bus deposit be made when the reservation was made. We then set out to collect and collected most of the mishandled monies. A check of company records revealed that charter sales were at a record high, the department was profitable, and complaints were at a record low during the years that I headed up the department.

Following the departure of the Senior Vice-President of Marketing, to whom I reported, I reported directly to the President (the same Assistant Regional Manager that I had inquired about when I saw him throwing packages around the inside of a freighter in 1962). Although I had invited him to our offices many times during my Vice-Presidency, he had come down only a couple of times. One morning in April 1983, he called me to his office and slammed the door, after I entered. He began to rave about a complaint received from the eastern part of the country. He was running around and raving about how it was handled. I told him that I had worked very hard to bring the department to the present level of performance that he hadn't even come to the department to understand the improvements that had been made, to acknowledge the improvements, and that he could not slam doors and shout at me – I wouldn't allow it. He appeared surprised and asked me what I said, and I repeated it. He said, "I made you a vice-president." I said, "I earned it." He said if that is how you feel, you are no longer a vice-president. You can go home, and someone will contact you. I went to my office, collected my personal items, told my staff that I had been relieved and went home.

Within a week, the president called me back to his office, told me that there were no positions open in Phoenix and showed me a list of positions available in the country. He knew that I had my family in Phoenix and owned several rental houses here. I had worked very closely with the personnel section when they developed the job categories and pay scale and understood the benefits of all the positions. He said "what?" when I said that I would accept the position of Regional Director, Jacksonville, Florida, responsible for all of Florida and Northern Georgia. It was the only reasonably midlevel position because I knew that my pay couldn't be lowered; the position provided a company car and that anytime that I was out of Jacksonville, I was on an expense account. "You will have to be there by the end of the week," he said. "I'll be there tomorrow," I replied. My wife had managed our home for most of the time that we had been married. I had spent many weeknights out of town on Greyhound business, now I would be away more weekends. Although I hated to leave my Cadillac, it often remained parked in the driveway.

I boarded a plane, arrived in Jacksonville the next evening and picked up my company full-sized Ford. I knew the drill, rented an apartment, shopped for the basics, TV, bedding, three pans, a couple of dishes, flatware, towels, etc. I set up my office, hired a secretary and begin to visit the terminals and offices in my area of responsibility. A few weeks after I arrived, I was told to turn my car in and purchase a new auto and selected a Buick. I knew most of the managers and some of the employees, which made it more comfortable. I was familiar with Florida and knew that it was deregulated, which allowed for pricing changes without regulatory approval. One of the first things that I did was to round up all ticket prices to the nearest quarter, which increased revenue. I had plans to eventually round up to the nearest dollar and eliminate all change. With all ticket prices in dollars, there was the possibility of using ticket-selling machines with bill accepters. I spent most of the time as Regional Director in the field, using the expense account to cover the additional expenses. I spent the Labor Day weekend (the last busy holiday) in Savanna, Georgia, returned to Jacksonville, resigned and returned home to my family in Phoenix.

I believed that Greyhound and I had been married long enough; it was time for a divorce!

PART FIVE
LIFE AFTER GREYHOUND

250

CHAPTER 17

SEEKING NEW OPPORTUNITIES

When I was in Jacksonville, Florida, I requested my wife, Wilda, to look for investment opportunities that might assist with expenses following my departure from Greyhound and until I found other employment. I thought that a laundromat would require less attention and maintenance, after it was properly equipped and decorated. Wilda located one on the Westside of Phoenix. We agreed to purchase it, after reviewing their profit and loss statement. When I returned to the city we repaired and replaced washers and added other equipment and painted it to enhance the place. We conducted marketing efforts in the neighborhood that included give-a-ways and refreshments. The schedule required that the place be opened early in the morning, kept open late and cleaned often. We increased the patronage, but we found out that the neighborhood was not an area that would allow profitability. Our machines were often broken and damaged. The coin collectors were also frequently damaged, as people tried to get the coins out or to operate the machines without paying. They left the space in need of constant cleaning and policing. I had people trying to show me how to run the machines without paying, not knowing that I owned the place. After several months and a couple of confrontations with people in the facility, Wilda convinced me that we should sell it before something serious happened. We covered our investment in the sale and moved on.

When I made the decision to leave Greyhound, I was not aware of the pending, if not already existing, economic recession. Companies were reducing their payroll, especially management personnel. I also found out that, due to my having been a vice-president of a major corporation, they would often not consider giving me an interview. I received responses that they couldn't meet my salary level or that they didn't have anything that I would be interested in. Additionally, there were only two major intercity bus companies (Motor Coach): Greyhound and Trailways, which was headed by the officers that I had left at Greyhound in 1979 and were trying to rebuild that company. I sent resumes to every company in the area that I could recall, answered many newspaper advertisements, followed-up on leads and consulted employment agencies to no avail. I applied to the local transit system, Phoenix Transit, on more than one occasion, and couldn't get a response or an interview.

Wilda and I established a corporation, U-Save Travel Club, Inc. I realized that with deregulation of the travel, entertainment and transportation industry, services would be marketed and sold directly to consumers. The strategy for the corporation was to obtain contracts with organizations that provided sleeping accommodations, attractions, entertainment, transportation and other services and to offer direct discounts to card-carrying members. The corporation would profit from membership fees and would offer tours and services directly to members at a reduced cost. The concept was sound, and the organizations responded with contracts and discounts. Our effort was great, but the program was too extensive for our limited budget, and when we made presentations in person, our color often reversed the original commitments that had been made. Although we revised and reduced the program, it was unsuccessful, and we lost a substantial amount of money. I believe that we were years before our time, as I observe companies such as Hotels.Com, Priceline, Hotwire and others that came later and are very profitable.

I registered with some temporary labor agencies and began working at whatever work I was offered. I drove trucks, cleaned warehouses, restocked stores, did inventory, made collections from coin-operated telephones, did product merchandising, manual labor and anything else that was legal and paid. Wilda went back to work for the first time since we were married, as a temporary clerical worker. In 1985, she was employed with the Glendale Union High School District. That provided the family with insurance and additional income. The only children in the house by then were Scott and Erika, both of whom were in school.

We began to seek out a new church home and came across a newspaper advertisement for Unity of Phoenix, which was within a few miles of our home. I had attended Unity of Detroit several times and I was familiar with "The Daily Word" magazine, which my mother always read. When I told Wilda that I was going to check it out, she said that we could both go and take the children. After attending several months, we all joined and have been members for over twenty years. Scott & Erika became active in the "Youth of Unity"' a program, which I (and they) credit with much of their future success and accomplishments.

Following the Sunday morning service in 1986, I purchased the book, *The Perfect "Power Within You"* by Jack Ensign Addington. The book contains a program that includes daily lessons and affirmations that instructs the reader how to bring about desired life changes. I followed the program, which challenged me to make some moves in a new direction. I left a steady temporary job and took a new job.

Within a short period of time, I received a call from a former Greyhound Lines Inc. associate, Vander Brown, who I had not talked to for years and who was then a President of a division. He requested that I come to San Francisco to assist him with a marketing program. His request was that I prepare a marketing program for Casino Service from the San Francisco Bay Area to Reno and Lake Tahoe. Our meeting was in spring 1986, and he wanted me to prepare the program for inclusion in the fall schedule, which was in September. When we met the next day, I told him that I wouldn't prepare a program for September because it would possibly fail, as that was the beginning of the slow season. In order for the program to have the best results, we would need to roll it out for the summer schedule change. In response to his concern that I could not have it ready within several weeks, I reminded him that God created the world in seven days; I surely could do this in several weeks.

Working out of an office that they provided me, I developed a marketing program built around the "Lucky Streak" casino program that I had worked on when employed with Greyhound. The fare structure was reviewed, and we changed the schedule to institute a half-hour service from the Bay Area to the Casinos. Coaches left for Reno on the hour and for Lake Tahoe on the half-hour from San Francisco, Oakland and points enroute. We had express coaches during primetime and local coaches where needed. The schedules direct to the casinos were evaluated and new casinos were added when they offered cash incentives to Greyhound passengers.

I developed a fun book that contained discounts and gifts to riders when they visited businesses in Reno and Lake Tahoe at a cost of printing only. Although I was told that it couldn't be done, I developed, instituted and monitored a "Frequent Rider Program," by offering membership cards to Casino passengers. When a passenger bought ten tickets and his card was stamped, they received a free round-trip ticket.

To introduce the new program, we developed a multimedia presentation that we took to the employees, agents and vendors. The program was kicked off with a special promotion to benefit a national charity and a news conference in San Francisco and Oakland. When persons questioned the number of tickets reportedly bought by some passengers, I took some company employees to ticket selling locations, and they confirmed that member passengers were in fact going to the casinos as many as thirty times a month, sometimes twice a day.

I then recommended that Greyhound consider introducing a new service route between Phoenix and Las Vegas, Nevada via Laughlin, Nevada. Although there was some resistance, the service that was instituted was one of the selected routes that operated later during a nationwide strike and is still in service as of this writing. I spent some time locating casinos that would participate in the program and arranging promotions in Laughlin and Las Vegas.

Following my presentation, a young manager at the Tropicana Hotel and Casino, Las Vegas, asked me if I didn't remember him, which I didn't. He told me that years earlier, I had interviewed him and gave him his first job out of college. He not only cooperated with our program, but he arranged for my wife and me to enjoy our seventeenth wedding anniversary, on October 29th, as guests of the hotel, including shows and meals.

The program that was outlined in the book, *"The Perfect Power Within You"*, proved to be an important instrument in assisting me in implementing all of the training, teachings, prayers, beliefs and faith that I had been exposed to over my lifetime. I recommend the book to everyone who is interested in improving his or her life and I have given dozens of copies as gifts. I have told friends and relatives that I consider the book as a handbook for planning, changing and improving their lives.

Wilda and I were dealing with the medical challenges that families with which chronic illness are confronted. We sought treatment for Erika's Cystic Fibrosis, a hereditary, chronic disease of the pancreas, lungs, etc. We became active in the Arizona Consortium for Children with Chronic Illness, an advocacy organization. I accepted the part-time position as Executive Administrator following the completion of my consulting assignment with Greyhound. The remainder of the time was spent attempting to market U-Save Travel Club.

In 1989, an associate of mine, a manager at Phoenix Transit, contacted me with an offer of a part-time supervisory job with the company. Following a short training session, I was employed as a Transit Supervisor, part time, at an hourly rate. Within months, I observed an advertisement for a marketing position that was posted, and I applied for it. The transportation department where I was assigned contacted me and offered me a job as an assistant to the manager responsible for driver dispatch and promised to match the money that the marketing position advertised. Following interviews and their expressed desire to keep me in the department on a full-time basis, I accepted.

I found the work environment to be the most hostile that I had known in my work experience of over fifty years. There appeared to be little or no respect among employees. Loud exchanges between managers and employees and contract employees would not be unusual. I attempted to establish a policy of respect by learning the names of as many employees as possible, as quickly as I could, while addressing them by name. I explained that I would meet with anyone at any time that I had available, upon request. Most of the supervisors and managers had risen through the ranks from bus operator and I was told that since I hadn't, I didn't know enough to supervise or correct them. Some went so far as to write to management and request that I be removed.

My manager was younger than I and was concerned that I was there to replace him. I explained to him, during the initial interview, that I was not interested in assuming more responsibility. My experience with Greyhound had satisfied any ambition that I had. I was there to assist and would use my experience to make him look good. After a couple of months, without any review or explanation, I arrived one morning to be met by my associate, the manager who recommended me and his counterpart, who without explanation removed me and reassigned me to a Transit Supervisory position. I made several requests for an explanation from my manager, the Director of Transportation and the personnel department, but never received it. I did not object to the reassignment, which was more to my liking, operating on my own, outside of the office, supervising operators, checking service, and investigating accidents.

This position was exempt from the shifts that were bid, with me being the low person on the seniority roster for some time. I learned most of the employees' names, especially those that I had contact with on a regular basis. I boarded as many buses as possible, introduced myself to the operators and offered any assistance needed. Although my effort was met with suspicion, I began to gain their respect and trust. To further distinguish myself from their thoughts about supervision, I purchased a large bag of Werther's Original candy and gave one to each operator with each visit. This became costly, but effective with me being able to advise operators that I was out there and observing them, by placing a piece of candy in their work area when they were off the bus. This exercise continued until I retired and when I meet any of them now, they still expect candy.

Four years after retiring, we were boarding an airplane in Chicago for Phoenix when I spoke to a Phoenix Transit Operator who was seated on board. He was glad to see me and after the greeting he said, "Fred, do you have candy for me?" When I reached in my pocket and gave it to him, he stood and told everyone on the plane how I had always looked out for him and carried candy that I gave to the operators.

In 1993, my manager, one of those who had walked me out of the assignment in the dispatch office, contacted me about a request that had been made for me to take a special assignment. He appeared unusually reluctant to ask me and said that he thought he knew what my answer was going to be. The former Phoenix Transit Director of Transportation and the manager that had arranged for my removal from the dispatch area, without explanation were now in Las Vegas, Nevada, establishing a new transit service for the parent company and requesting that I come there and train new transit supervisors. My initial thought was "Hell no!" That evening I was telling Wilda about them having the nerve to make the request when she said, "Fred, you know that you are a better person than they are, why don't you go and show them? Besides, you might enjoy doing something different." I thought about it and wondered how they would act when I accepted. I did explain to them that the job couldn't be done properly in a week, that I would spend two weeks. They were very humble and gracious, providing me with a rental car and good accommodations. I stayed three weeks, trained the supervisors, and assisted with forms, procedures, operator contacts and the layout of the new facility.

While out with the new supervisors, I learned that the supervisors who had visited Phoenix had returned to Las Vegas and told them that they didn't want to be sent back to Phoenix for training; that they learned something only while working with me and I should be brought to Las Vegas to train them. When I completed the assignment, they paid me a small bonus and gave me an award expressing their thanks. On the way home, I stopped in Los Angeles to visit my son, Scott. We shopped for a more reliable used car, donating the bonus money for the down payment and we had dinner.

Early in 1995, I began to talk to employees about establishing an employee club. In May, I posted a notice over my name, no job title, on several company bulletin boards proposing and outlining the establishment of an employee club. The purpose, membership, conditions, administration, dues and method of raising funds were included. I also included proposals for social activities, member emergency loans and employee assistance during illness and emergencies. I requested that employees interested in assisting, joining, or becoming board members sign an accompanying sheet. Some of the first notes and comments that were recorded were profane and or very negative. I took the sheets down and posted new ones. From over nine hundred employees, I was able to obtain over seventy people who signed as interested in becoming members. Eight expressed an interest in being board members. The initial joining fee was $10 for the year with half of the money raised being raffled back to new members who could donate it back to the club if they wished. Although it was not my intention at the beginning, I accepted the position of President and held it for two years. We started with a couple hundred members, an annual picnic, a

Christmas party and a motor coach trip to the casinos in Laughlin, Nevada, which I arranged and hosted.

I introduced a "Golden Angel Membership" for employees agreeing to pledge $1.00 or more per paycheck. The company agreed to allow operators to wear the small golden angel pins on their uniform. We went on to establish the member loan program, a club food bank, and a monthly food bank through Saint Mary's Food Bank where food boxes could be bought at a discount and formed a scholarship program for employee's children. When I left office, the organization had approximately $20,000 in assets. It is my understanding that the program is still in existence at Phoenix Transit.

Late in 1997 or early 1998, I sat in a supervisor's meeting, during which the General Manager told the Assistant General Manager of Transportation that he was directing him to reorganize the department into work teams, develop a program with team leaders and team meetings, and to identify results and improvements. He publicly announced that failure to have this done within an established period would result in management changes. The General Manager who made the demand had recently been in the Assistant Manager's position and had not implemented the program. The teams would consist of operators who worked 4, 5, 6 and sometimes 7 days on shifts starting at approximately 2 AM until 6 PM, lasting up to ten hours, some with split-shifts. Basically, this was an impossible thing to do, and what I thought was that it was an effort to terminate the only black Assistant General Manager, who had more time in grade than the General Manager, who may have seen him as a threat.

I watched and listened. As the time passed, the supervisors discussed that it was almost impossible to develop the program and what was going to happen. Three-quarters of the way through the given period for the development of the program, I visited the Assistant General Manager and asked him if he was working on the program. He said he didn't have the knowledge or experience to do it and was looking into ways to get it done. I said, "Do you know that he intends to fire you if you don't get it done?" and he replied, "Yes." I said, "Time is running out," and I started to leave. He asked me if I knew how to develop the program and I said I hadn't given it much thought; it wasn't my problem, but I was sure that it could be done. He asked me if I would work on it, and I agreed to think about it. I considered the challenge and, despite the fact that I didn't want to work out of an office, I told him that I would do it, with the support and commitment from the General Manager and his staff. We had lunch with the General Manager and his assistant, where I outlined how I thought the program could be done, but only if they promised to support it.

My concern was based on the fact that I had seen too many programs and projects started and allowed to die because they were not given proper support. Following the assurance that the program was a new direction for the department and that top management would support it, I came off the road assignment and went into the office. I agreed to establish the program and I told everyone that I would not remain in the position to administer the program beyond the first cycle or bid period. I reminded management that someone needed to review and understand the procedure and method that I was using in order to reset the schedules and meetings. Although I had not requested or expected any additional benefits, I was given a new title consistent with the work that I was doing – Coordinator or Supervisor of Teams – or something to that effect. The company also gave me an increase in salary as the plans for the program developed. Within the allowed period and before the deadline issued by the General Manager, I developed the team program, assigned all operators to teams, assigned team leaders, outlined the meeting, agenda, and scheduled meetings for the operator to bid upon the period in effect.

The program required that I schedule a meeting around the check-in time for as many operators as possible, arrange for the relief of operators on their runs, arrange for them to be sent out to their bus at the end of each meeting, and assign a supervisor team leader to conduct each meeting. When it was not possible to assign operators at time of check in, I had to assign them to a team and arrange for them to be relieved from a run as close to one of two training facilities, at the most convenient time, and arrange for their return following each meeting. The team leaders were directed to make contact with their members several times during the month, in addition to the meetings, and to record activities. The program required more direct contact with the supervisors and the operators, resulting in more interaction among operators, correcting some operating problems, and improving morale.

Although I had advised that the cost would be great before developing the program, the company was not supportive of it once they determined the amount of the additional costs. When we were nearing the completion of the first session (operator bid period), I requested that I be relieved and returned to my regular assignment. There was no one who understood how the program was created, administrated or able to reconstruct it. They requested that I reset the program for the next operator bid and assured me that they would bring in another person to replace me before the next bid. I agreed and I supervised the program through the next bid, during which I experienced the declining support for the program. They brought in another transit supervisor, who had been with the company much longer than I had been and who had been promoted to supervision after I joined the company. I welcomed him into the job and offered to explain the program and assist him in any way that he needed. He assured me that he didn't need any help; he could handle it. During an orientation meeting, I would have explained that the program was doomed to failure because the manager no longer supported it, had he listened. I returned to the Transit Supervisor position and left him to handle the program.

On a Monday evening in 1997, following an inspiring Sunday, Unity of Phoenix Church message that said: "With God as my protector, of whom should I be afraid, what should I fear?" I found myself thinking about this over and over. If you understand this and believe this, what if anything should you fear? I was working as a Transit Supervisor, driving north on Central Avenue in a Specially equipped Dodge Caravan. The van was radio equipped and contained tools, spare parts and mirrors that we used to replace broken bus mirrors, make minor repairs that were loosely onboard. The van had Captain-style front seats with a high headrest on the back. As I approached Van Buren Road, the light was green, and I looked to left for oncoming traffic and then to the right.

I saw a large white pickup truck approaching the intersection at a high rate of speed and knew that I was going to be hit. I can't explain why but I felt no fear or concern; but there seemed to have been a sudden feeling of a wrap or large hand around my body and I was sure that I was going to be ok. The van was struck on the right rear corner, which caused it to flip into the air and land upside down on the top. I remember sliding down Central Avenue for a couple of hundred feet, with glass breaking sparks flying, smoke coming from the engine area, and items flying round the inside of the van. However, I felt relaxed and fearless in whatever was surrounding me.

When the van came to a stop, some young people who were walking in the area ran over to get me out of the smoking van. I was hanging upside down with my seatbelt still attached as they tried to pull me out. I asked them to stop pulling so that I could release the belt and I then dropped into the van's ceiling, rolled out the door and walked over to the curb. The Phoenix Fire department arrived very quickly, checked the van for other passengers and started to check me out. They took my blood pressure and it was normal. They looked shocked, so they cleared the equipment and took it again. The only injury was a small cut on my hand that I believe I got crawling out of the van. I couldn't understand how I had not suffered head injuries or a broken neck. I went back to look at the van the following day at the garage where it was towed. Employees came over and asked me who had been killed and who was driving. When I said, "I was", they couldn't understand how I was ok. I couldn't explain it, other than to tell them about the hand or whatever I felt around me at the time I was hit!

I didn't understand the message from Sunday, I kept wondering in my mind how it worked, God gave me a demonstration!

Within months, the program was in fast decline and the new supervisor was extremely frustrated. At one point, he had a medical episode on the job and was rushed to the hospital because they thought he was having a heart attack. I was nearing retirement and was surprised when the personnel department contacted me and told me that they planned to reduce my salary by the amount that they had raised it to when I was developing the program. The company history, which supported my position, said that no supervisor's salary could be reduced when he left a position on good terms. I appealed to the General Manager by asking him if he thought that I was a good employee and if he thought that this action was fair. I had received awards for Supervisor of the Month, the Quarter and the Year, along with other awards.

Following our meeting, my salary was not interrupted, and I received an annual increase. Approaching my sixty-fifth birthday, I submitted retirement papers. I witnessed the frustration of the supervisor, as he attempted to administer the team program that was not being supported. I was concerned about his health, if he continued to perform the impossible task of successfully administering the program, and/or if he were returned to a Transit Supervisor position without understanding what had happened. I contacted him through the company radio system and arranged to meet him in a downtown parking lot. He arrived, wondering why I had requested the meeting, and somewhat suspect of my purpose. I explained that it was my concern for his health and his future. I explained the history of the program, how it had drifted in the direction that it had, the lack of knowledge and support that the managers had given it and that it was doomed for failure before he took the assignment. I went further and expressed my concern for his health, his family's welfare and suggested that he consider retiring. We reviewed several possibilities for him to support himself and family, including him joining his wife in her job. I believe that he heard and understood me because I was told within two days that he was retiring before me.

Wilda and I were in a store in Phoenix several months later, and after a chance meeting with a smiling gentleman who said that he was now working with his wife, I explained to her that this was the person that I thought was going to die on the job if I didn't convince him to retire. Prior to my retirement, one of the managers who walked me out of the position in the dispatch department was offered a lesser position and left the company. The second manager involved was also offered a lesser position and was suffering from anxiety. He became ill on the job and was taken to the hospital. I spoke with him about retiring before he had more serious medical problems and he accepted my advice and retired. The Assistant General Manager accepted a more desirable position and he left the company.

On November 29, 1999, a date that I once thought was forever coming, I retired from Phoenix Transit, received the watch, other gifts and a pension. Following my lead, Wilda retired from the Glendale Union High School District in May 2001, and we used the experience that we obtained by practicing retirement to travel and enjoy life. We visited Europe, with stops in Paris, Berlin, and Amsterdam.

On a very hot day, during the summer of 2002, I was driving on 35th Avenue and passed a woman sitting on a power scooter in the hot sun. When I passed her, I thought that she might need help, but she was on the other side of the street, and I kept driving. In the next block I turned around because my intuition told me she needed help. I approached her carefully after parking my car and asked if she had a problem. Her battery had run out of power and she couldn't move. I knew that there was a Fry's Food store about two blocks away and I pushed her to the store as she sat on the scooter. I transferred her to one of the store's electric shopping carts and told her to do her shopping while I tried to arrange for her to get home.

When I worked at Phoenix Transit, field supervisors drove vans that were equipped to haul wheelchairs and scooters. I contacted their dispatch office, talked to someone that I knew and was told that they no longer had them in service. I obtained the help of a store manager who ran an extension cord outside where I could plug the scooter in to recharge it. When the woman finished shopping, we placed her and her groceries on her scooter and I told her that I would follow her in my car until she arrived home, which was about 8 blocks away. After two blocks, the scooter quit again.

I parked my car and began pushing her, on the scooter with groceries towards her house. It was very hot, around 115 degrees and the pavement was hot. I was surprised that I could only push for about a half block before I was out of breath, but I assumed that it was the heat and the load that I was pushing. I was able to get her home where she thanked me and gave me some cold water.

On the morning of January 2, 2003, I awoke with a pain on the left side of my back. I had Wilda put some rubbing alcohol on it and thought that it would be okay. When it didn't get better, Wilda insisted that I see a doctor or go to the hospital emergency room. I didn't think that it was anything to worry about, but to keep the peace, I agreed to let her take me to Thunderbird Banner Hospital. When we entered the hospital, she told the attendant that she thought I was having a heart attack. They began to work on me immediately, although I thought that they were over-reacting. They ran several tests, and later that evening, the doctors told Wilda and me that I had blockage in five arteries and that I needed open heart surgery.

I remembered that I had told Wilda, following her father's very difficult heart surgery, that I didn't believe I could handle such surgery. The second thing I recalled was that I had expressed to several friends, months earlier, that I had lived long enough to appreciate everything that had happened to me in my life. Was I going to appreciate this? I could only smile and say 'yes'. The third thing that I thought of was, through the Grace of God, I had not died that hot day while pushing that scooter. I underwent a bypass on five (5) arteries. Since I'm writing this in 2009, the operation was a success and I enjoy an active lifestyle.

We made frequent trips to Laughlin, NV for a couple of days of rest and recuperation. We visited friends and family members around the country and when we were not traveling, we relaxed and entertained in our home in Phoenix. "Life was Good, All was Well, and We were Blessed".

CHAPTER 18

FAMILY

Family has always been important to me. During my teenage years, I often thought how great it would be to have a wife and children to love, and for which to provide. I studied my family and made note of the things that I appreciated and things that I didn't like about the inter-relationships between family members. My experience with courting was limited as a teenager, due to my working while going to school. When I was eighteen, I decided to leave home and see first-hand what the remainder of the world lived like outside of Saginaw and Detroit, Michigan.

My first stop was Cleveland, Ohio, where I lived and worked for several months. Through much of my childhood, I lived in a home where there were roomers that were not family members and I disliked the idea that I would and could meet people that I didn't know in the house, from time to time. But living in a large rooming house in Cleveland, Ohio, where I was one of several other adults and two children was enlightening. I learned to respect and to live with other people, outside of family members, where my family was not in the majority. I also confirmed that I was capable of living on my own as a responsible adult.

When I returned to Detroit, the only family that I had was the one that I left there. My next move was to join the U.S. Army and I found a very large family, some loveable, some respectful, but an experience that included a diverse population of colors, races, sizes and personalities from around the country. I learned a great deal from that early experience, and even more as I became an officer and assumed responsibility for the lives of other men, some younger, but mostly older than myself. This was also my first experience living in the South and I began making adjustments for it.

Army life has a way of putting a damper on romantic relationships. In the military, you are not a resident for any period of time and available singles know that you are here today, gone tomorrow. During basic training, advanced basic and during Officer's Candidate School, I spent my time trying to move into the officer ranks, as soon as possible. Upon graduation in March 1955, I was shipped to Salzburg, Austria, where even the coolest white officers couldn't get a date. We spent hours drinking, playing pool and admiring the one attractive waitress at the officer's club.

It has been over fifty years, but I don't recall any other Negro officers in Salzburg. You could look, admire, drink and eat, but no dating in Salzburg, Austria, when I was there.

I traveled to Frankfurt, Germany, by rail enroute to Berlin with a one-night layover. Not knowing what to expect when I arrived behind the "Iron Curtain," I decided to have a last fling of freedom before going behind it. After visiting several drinking establishments, I settled in a club with a young, gorgeous blond. I was spending rather loosely and drinking more than I should have, while receiving encouragement and promises of close companionship as the night went on. I should have known that she was not drinking as much as I was buying, but Richard Pryor said, and he was right, that stuff makes you "null and void". When the dawn broke and I started to clear my head, I found myself alone and with a lot less Deutsche Marks. A well-learned lesson was received that night and many "Bar Girls" have approached me over the years and they got nothing.

On my birthday many years later, in Cincinnati, Ohio, at a Hustler Club, in response to requests for drinks, I passed out cigars to the Bar Girls and had them all smoking them until the manager came over and asked them if they had lost their minds. Cigars was the most they could get.

When I arrived in Berlin, after riding through the Russian Zone by rail with all of the windows covered, I was surprised to find a beautiful lively city full of attractive young ladies, many of which were friendly. Life was good and I soon moved into a three-bedroom flat, complete with everything except food, drinks and music--and I soon took care of that. I had a roommate for a short period of time, but he was soon shipped to a new assignment in Western Germany. The Army claimed that it was integrated, but while other white officers lived in crowded quarters designed for no more than three, I continued to live alone in my 3-bedroom flat until they built new quarters, over a year later. They were welcome to visit, and I cooked dinner and had parties where all were invited, but they couldn't get assigned to my flat. My flat was warm and very friendly, and I entertained many German females. When Ed (E.J.) Nichols came to visit from Western Germany, where he was a student, he introduced me to a young black female exchange student. We had a very close relationship and spoke of marriage, but she told me that she didn't want children and I did. She returned to the states and I met several other young females. Most of the relationships were those where we went to restaurants, clubs or spent time at my quarters.

When I met Vera Swartz, we started in the same manner, but shortly afterward, she invited me to meet her family. My German was limited, and she spoke English, but her family spoke only German. I was able to understand, very early in the relationship that I was welcome in the home by the whole family, including parents, grandparents, aunts, uncles, cousins and other relatives. I soon had a new family and we spent much time together at dinners, family functions and during holidays.

In December 1956, I asked Vera to marry me; she accepted, and we submitted the request for approval to get married. We were married in February 1957. Although Vera told me later that she couldn't have children, she became pregnant in June and our first daughter, Denise Renee, was born in Detroit, Michigan on March

28, 1958. Our second daughter, Monique Yvette was born on December 2, 1960. Our son Frederick Jr. was born on July 24, 1961, in Detroit, Michigan.

The marriage was good and working well in Berlin. Returning to Detroit from Berlin, Germany, our relationship began to dissolve, due to financial, family and cultural problems. In retrospect, my marriage in 1958 was a move of the heart, many years before its time. The marriage was in great danger after I made the move back to the United States.

In 1962 the marriage ended, although the divorce didn't come until 1963. I assumed the role of both parents, and Vera went about her business. Following a brief and difficult struggle in Detroit with the children, and with no support from Vera or my family, I moved the children and myself to Cleveland, Ohio, and found work. The details of our life, with me as both parents, are outlined in other chapters.

We survived, and in 1969 I was rewarded with a loving wife, Wilda, a partner, and soulmate. And again, I have enjoyed the love and support of her family; two additional loving children and seven grandchildren.

A family picture, which appears in the photograph section of this book, was taken in 2008 following the "Bowman Annual Christmas Brunch." The brunch has been a family tradition for more than twenty-five years. Wilda and I begin planning and buying for this shortly after each brunch and lately we find ourselves questioning if we are still able to prepare for and entertain upwards of 80 guests each Christmas Day between the hours of 10:00AM and 2:00PM. It had been such an important part of our life and the lives of family member and friends that it was hard to consider stopping. We prepared and served waffles, fried chicken, hash brown potatoes, biscuits, eggs, bacon, sausage, donut holes, juice, coffee and fruit. Friends that attended for years brought their grandchildren and, if we continued, we would meet their great-grandchildren. Our granddaughter was so proud of the family tradition that she wrote about it for a class assignment. If we were to stop the affair, we would have to send out information to family and friend that we were no longer having it. We didn't have to send out invitations because people knew that on Christmas Day, between 10AM and 2PM they could eat, laugh and gain fellowship in our home.

My family now includes many, many people that have been a part of my life during the past seventy-three years: **GOD,** friends, foes, family members, acquaintances, associates and strangers that provided me with experiences that molded me into the person that I have become. For this, I am grateful, I am blessed! I am grateful that I was able to provide the commitment and the effort that it took to keep the family together during the time that I was an only parent, and for the effort that their Stepmother made in providing them with everything that they needed to guide them to the successful lives that they now enjoy.

CHAPTER 19

YEARS LATER
IN THE BIG APPLE

On Tuesday, June 24, 2008, Wilda and I boarded Delta Airlines flight 640 enroute to New York City. This flight was a "redeye" leaving Phoenix at 11:15 PM and arriving in NYC at 07:05AM. It had been years since I had taken an overnight flight, and as I remember, the last one that I took was between Phoenix and NYC.

That red-eye flight is one that I remember well. *It was one of the most difficult assignments that I had during my career with Greyhound Lines. I had recommended and obtained the approval to close the New York office of Greyhound Charter Services. We were in the process of reorganizing and transferring all charter sales and processing to our Phoenix office to improve efficiency and save costs. It was my responsibility and I chose to tell the employees that they were going to lose their jobs. My eight years' experience in the Industrial Relations Department, which included many hearing and court cases involving terminations, taught me that you expose the company to complaints and other legal actions when you*

278

try to protect certain employees in a non-union office, where seniority is not a factor. I knew that the best management action was to terminate everyone and close the office that was located in the high rent area of Rockefeller Center.

Upon arrival that morning, I felt a little ill. I skipped breakfast and went directly to the NYC office. I began by telling the manager, who I had not told in advance because I was sure that he would tell some of the other employees. He expressed concern for some of the older employees and those that were performing well. I expressed my sympathy for them yet explained that we could consider rehiring some of them in other locations or other positions within the company at a later time. The news was taken hard and it was all that I could do to maintain my composure. I answered as many questions as possible, explained the company policy regarding terminations, severance pay, and other benefits when closing the office.

I returned to Phoenix that evening and met with my supervisor, the Senior Vice-President of Marketing, who had approved the closing. To my dismay he told me that I lacked interpersonal relations skills, in that I had terminated certain employees that the office manager desired to reassign. He placed a notation in my personal file to that effect. It was not because of anything that I did or that he did to me, but he was terminated by the company several months later.

During the flight back to NYC with Wilda, I remembered that incident, the many hotel nights that I spent in the city away from my family, the many decisions that I made there, the people that I met, the challenges and the enjoyment that the city had given me over the years.

It had been only a year earlier that we had traveled to Atlanta, Georgia for the graduation of our oldest grandson, Justin Bayless. He had graduated from the prestigious Morehouse College with honors. As a sophomore he had been inducted into the Phi Beta Kappa Honor Society in May 2005.   His guests at graduation had noted that his name had not been listed with those receiving such honors, although he had the honor ropes. I pointed out that they did not have a listing for sophomores, only juniors and seniors. Justin was already in New York finishing his one-year work assignment with Morgan Stanley. He was returning to Phoenix to become CFO at Michael B. Bayless and Associates, P.C., his father's company.

On Wednesday morning June 25, 2008, Wilda and I were there for a more enjoyable and festive occasion. We were being rewarded for the many hours that we spent attending pre-school, grade school and high school activities along with sport events where our second oldest grandson, Jerryd Bayless, participated. We were there to witness and support him and his family when he was drafted as a player into the National Basketball Association.   Jerryd was included in a select group of top prospects that were honored because they were expected to be in the NBA Draft Lottery.

We arrived in time to join our daughter and enjoy breakfast, compliments of the NBA. Jerryd joined us later and we wished him well during the following evening, when the Draft would be held at Wamu Theater, Madison Square Garden. We were staying at the Westin NYC Times Square, which was the NBA host hotel. There were a host of NBA personnel, past and present NBA players, the media people, top prospects for the 2008 draft and others included in the one hundred players from U.S. colleges and institutions, along with international players.

That afternoon we were sitting in the lobby and I was observing the fans, players, prospects, family members and the staff of the hotel. The high number of African Americans in the hotel and the area struck me. It was pretty much commonplace to most of the young people that were moving about. But it reminded me of the fact that in 1941, my father, Rev. William Bowman, Sr. and an interracial group of representatives from the United Auto Workers Union made reservations at one of New York City's finest hotels. The black members of the group were denied accommodations. The entire group, including the white members who had been pre-registered, moved to another hotel. My father took the rejection personally and initiated legal action in a 1942 civil case and received an award that opened public accommodations in the state of New York.

The highlight of the evening was a dinner party honoring Jerryd, two other top prospects and their families, which had the same Sports Agent as he had. We enjoyed a great meal, fellowship, and had a chance to take some memorable pictures. On Thursday June 26th we enjoyed breakfast again, complements of the NBA. There were activities for the top prospects and their parents. Wilda and I enjoyed meeting and talking to family members of other future NBA players. Following lunch, we prepared for the main event, the 2008 National Basketball Association Draft. Wilda and I made sure that we were dressed appropriately, but that we were also comfortable.

There was a fleet of buses lined up outside of the host hotel for top prospects, their families and invited friends that would take us to Madison Square Garden where the NBA Draft was to be held. Aboard the bus, the atmosphere was electrical and exciting, with everyone aboard holding hopes for their favorite prospect to be drafted early in the draft. Jerry had been projected as high as fifth, but some of the late information indicated that he would be drafted eleventh.

The crowd at the Garden was large and the lines were long. We were able to meet our other family members in the crowd. Scott, my youngest son went ahead and secured seats for the family members that were not in the section reserved for the top prospects, parents and close friends. This was an exciting and wonderful experience for Wilda and me, having watched Jerryd from birth grow into a young man and an accomplished basketball player, now being considered for one of the only four hundred plus team player positions in the NBA. We recall how he had said that he would play in the NBA, when he was a kid playing pee-wee basketball. The family watched and cheered as the first ten draft prospects were announced. When Jerryd Bayless was announced as the eleventh pick of the Indiana Pacers, in the 2009 NBA Draft, the family and his other supporters broke into loud applauses.

I thought about the many days that I had spent in Indianapolis, a great distance from Phoenix. The weather in Indianapolis and the fact that I didn't believe that it was a good place for him, was on my mind. Within a few minutes, my son Scott received a text message that Jerryd had been traded to The Portland Trail Blazers. My first thought was that I had just taken a picture of the Trail Blazers banner that was hanging at the end of the row of seats where we were seated. My second thought was of a business trip I made in 1983, to call on the Portland Trail Blazers. It was the last official act as Vice-President, Charter Services, Greyhound Line, Inc. As I end this chapter, I have had the experience of watching Jerryd in 53 games, this NBA regular season, and one in his first two playoff games. I am proud that he is living his dream!

CHAPTER 20

FORTY-SEVEN YEARS LATER

On Friday March 6, 2009, Wilda and I were returning home from running errands, when she used her cellular phone to check the home phone for messages. When she finished, she said that there was a message from Delphenia with a telephone number for me to call her. Although reserved in her announcement, she knew what this meant to me. I had been attempting to locate Delphenia for years. That attempt had been intensified with the writing of this manuscript, "Shoulders". Every visit I made to Detroit, over the last several years, included some effort to locate her or someone who knew her. I had enlisted the help of relatives in the area and searched public records of births, marriages, divorces, and deaths, to no avail.

During a visit by a grandniece, last year, I told her the story of how Delphenia had been an important part of my life when I became the only parent of three infants, due to my wife choosing to leave the four of us and to satisfy her self-interests. I told her that I had tried many ways to reach her, but to no avail. We discussed my need for someone to do some leg work for me in the Detroit area. One of the limiting factors was the limited amount of information that I had

284

about Delphenia, her family, background, past addresses, or schools that she had attended. The only real clue that I had was a forty-seven-year-old picture of her. I told Chantel, my grandniece, that I would send her a copy of the picture and the little information that I had. I also told her that I would be willing to pay for a classified advertisement in a Detroit newspaper, if it wasn't too expensive.

Shortly after receiving the picture and information Chantel called me with information and the costs for local newspapers. We agreed that the best results would probably be obtained if we ran the "picture and a request for anyone knowing this person" to contact me. We chose the Michigan Chronicle, an African American publication, founded in 1936, which was also a newspaper that I sold in Detroit as a preteen. She also gave me the name and telephone number of the representative at the paper. Ms. Johnson, the representative, was very helpful during several phone calls, e-mails and faxes. We agreed to run the advertisement March 4th through March 10th. She wished me luck in locating Delphenia and she agreed to send me a tear-sheet that contained the advertisement. This was one of the best investments that I have made in a while.

Within hours after the newspaper hit the streets, her sister saw the picture and called her. Her niece also responded via e-mail, with a telephone number for Delphenia and herself. That evening, I was able to telephone Delphenia at her home in Birmingham, Michigan and we renewed our friendship. I was pleased that she thought enough to tell me of her surprise that I had been trying to locate her, and that I even used the newspaper as a source. She told me that her only daughter and her husband had made their transition. She also said that she had operated her own business for some thirty years. I was also able to tell her some of the stories that had developed since the weekend in 1962, when I came back to Detroit to move the children to Cleveland, a step ahead of Child Protection Service. We agreed to stay in touch. I sent her pictures of my present family taken in December 2008, along with pictures of the three children that she had cared for 47 years ago.

Wilda and I planned a trip back east the following summer and when in Detroit, visited with Delphenia.

IN CONCLUSION
I BELIEVE

Ihave now lived long enough to appreciate all of the things **that have happened to me in my lifetime!** There have been many good times, many bad times, and many painful and sad times when I didn't know how to understand or accept what was happening to me and around me at the time. There were times when I thought that the God I worshiped had forsaken or abandoned me, or never knew that I was alive. I spent times wondering what I had done to bring my life to the point that it was and if I would ever be able to return my life back to a point where I could enjoy it. The fact was that if there was any leaving done, it was I that did the leaving! Little did I know that all of this, every experience, was the making of Frederick Eloy Bowman, Sr.

When I was able to appreciate all of the things that I have experienced in my life, I learned who I am… I am a wonderful, unique, exciting, loving creation of God. I have never been anything less… I just didn't know it or forgot it from time to time. I am the co-creator of everything that I desire in my life. I am blessed with the Grace of God. I didn't earn it, didn't even request it … it came with the package at birth. It took me a long time (many years) to realize that it was always there and how great and powerful it is. Yes, grace is yours also and it is free!

Having said all of this, I believe that, through and with the power of Almighty God, I can do or have anything that my heart desires. Yes, I prove it every day. I am blessed with love, joy, health, happiness, prosperity, everything that I need and most of the things that I think that I want. Life is good. "It is All Good". I Thank God, yes, everyday!

I believe that all people are creations of God. Everyone was born by God and with His grace. We all have the ability to co-create what and how our lives develop. I believe that most of us, as I did, live for a long time without knowing this, if we ever learn it. It is easy to feel sorry for ourselves and to blame others for our lack of love, joy, happiness or prosperity, especially if you don't understand how to bring about change. Many of us were raised to believe that we don't deserve better, that we are not worthy of better. When we understand "grace", not earned but given at birth by a loving creator, we understand our worth. Love is the most powerful word in any language. Grace is love given in action and shown. You came with it – you can't dissolve it; you can't do anything so despicable that you lose it and it is yours until death. With such a wonderful, powerful gift, you had better learn to use and enjoy it.

I believe that we all know right from wrong. Judgment is something that comes with the package. We can exercise it improperly and say that we didn't know, but I believe that we do. There is something in me that tells me what is right and what is wrong. I decide whether I am going to do the right or wrong thing. Sometimes I do the right thing, other times I don't, but I always know what is right and what is wrong.

Intuition is a powerful gift that comes with the package. You can ignore it like the alarm clock in the morning. Most times, there is a penalty if you ignore either. Intuition may come as a gentle nudge, a small reminder, and a reoccurring thought. Many times, the penalty for ignoring your intuition can be life-changing. One example: In October 1980, my wife and I were attending a reception in a large hall in Manila, Philippines, where President Marcos was just beginning to speak. We were seated in the center of the hall, after having gone through a metal detector and body search and listening to several speakers praise President Marcos. My intuition caused me to feel uncomfortable, so I stood up and told my wife that I wanted to leave. President Marcos stopped speaking and my wife tried to get me to sit back down. I insisted, and we left the hall after explaining to some guards that we were returning to our hotel. My wife suggested that we wait on the tour bus that brought us to the affair, but I insisted on our taking a taxi (Jeep) back to the hotel. When we arrived at the hotel, Wilda asked me again if I was okay because she said that, unlike me, I had not been polite to the driver and was acting strangely. In the hotel room, I turned on the TV to watch the Baseball World Series and fixed us a cold drink. The announcer interrupted the Series with a report that a bomb had exploded at the reception that we had just left. We found out from other delegates returning late that night that the explosion that injured attendees was in the seating area where we left earlier and that we would have been injured or killed if we had been there. We were able to reserve a flight from the Philippines in the early morning hours to go to Hong Kong. Although we lost all of the pictures taken during our stops in Hawaii and Tokyo, Japan that we had placed in the photo shop in Manila, we were safe.

Love is the most precious, most sought after commodity in the world. The one item that the world needs more of is love. Everyone wants it, those that have it to give are sometimes afraid to give it and some of those that are being offered it, are afraid or don't know how to accept it. We should start to look into people's eyes, the "window to their soul," and quit looking away from people or looking at their bodies (their case). Imagine--visualize what would happen if everyone were to accept that we are all precious, loveable, equal creations of a loving, generous creator and that there is more than enough of everything in the world for everyone. There would be no need to hate, suppress, hurt, kill or withhold love from anyone. There would be no need to reject love or to be afraid that we would be hurt. If we were to remove suppression, hate, hurt and murder, and pour in love, what a wonderful world it would be!

I believe that most of the world's problems could be solved if each person would assume responsibility for him or herself and exercise self-control. God gave each of us free will and some conditions or commandments to follow. When all expectations of self-control are removed from society, when all responsibility for one's actions are dismissed, when everyone has the right to do as they please, individual desires take precedence over the needs and welfare of humankind. Safety, peace, happiness, progress and prosperity can only exist and grow in an environment where there is responsibility and self-control. When each person finally accepts responsibility for his or herself, exercises self-control and respects the rights and needs of others, there will not be a need for enforcements, imprisonment, or punishment. God provides for the needs of every person and everything that He created. We need only to be responsible for and care for what is provided. I believe that "There Is Only One Presence and One Power in the Universe: God the Good Omnipotent". Feel the Power, enjoy the Power. "The Power is Within You".

In order to heal, you must first forgive. I had been taught about forgiveness over the years yet failed to understand that it is the only way that you can be healed or be set free. When you allow yourself to carry the burden of anger, pain, distrust or unpleasant memories, you block the healing process and are never free from the experience. I carried the pain of having my first wife abandon the children and me for over twenty years while she went about her life. When I followed my teaching to release and forgive, I wrote her a letter. I told her that I forgave her for all and anything that she had done and asked her to forgive me for any contribution that I had made to the dissolution of the relationship. I further resolved that I was forgiving myself for all and anything that I had done in my life and resolved to try to live my life as best I could. This act of forgiveness allowed me to heal and it truly set me free!

ABOUT THE AUTHOR

FREDERICK E. BOWMAN
(fredwildabowan@aim.com)

JOB OBJECTIVE: A POSITION IN PHOENIX, ARIZONA, WHERE PAST EDUCATION AND EXPERIENCE MAY BE UTILIZED IN A CHALLENING AND REWARDING CAREER WITH OPPORTUNITY FOR ADVANCEMENT.

PERSONAL: Born: November 29, 1934, Saginaw, Michigan
Height: 6'3"
Weight: 210 lbs.
Marital Status: Married - two minor children
Health: Excellent

EDUCATION: Northern High School, Detroit, Michigan - Graduated 1952
Class President - Commander of R.O.T.C. - Public Speaking
Graduated in upper 25% of class

University of Detroit, Detroit, Michigan - 1952-1954
Pre-Legal Courses

MILITARY: U.S. Army - 1954-1958 - Honorable Discharge as 1st Lt.
Officer's Candidate School, Ft. Benning, Georgia:
* Food Management
* Military Instruction
* Logistics Planning and Management
* Military Justice System - Defense and Trial Counsel
Taught in NCO Academy, Berlin, Germany
Unit Commander and Staff Officer - Battalion and Regimental levels in Berlin, Germany, and Ft. Riley, Kansas
Basic training in Ft. Smith, Arkansas
Motor Officer and Food Management Officer
Ran Motor Pool of 150 vehicles and large Mess Hall for 700-800 people with 50 military and civilian employees

EXPERIENCE: GREYHOUND LINES, INC. - 1962-1983

April, 1983
to
September, 1983 Regional Director - Jacksonville, Florida
Duties and Responsibilities:
* Responsible for Greyhound operations in State of Florida and Southern Georgia
* Responsible for scheduling, pricing, sales, marketing, operations
* Three District Managers reported to me - eight major terminals (over 100 agencies)
* Reported to Regional Vice President in Atlanta, Georgia
Reason for leaving: Desire to return to Phoenix, Arizona, to rejoin my family.

FREDERICK E. BOWMAN   Page 2

EXPERIENCE
CONTINUED:

February, 1980   <u>Vice President, Charter Service</u> - Phoenix, Arizona
     to   Duties and Responsibilities:
April, 1983   * Directed activities of Charter Service Department
                          with sales volume of over $90 million
                        * Directed staff of approximately 20 people and
                          Charter Service Sales Offices consisting of 14 offices
                        * Established policy, procedures, pricing of rates,
                          advertising and promotion for all Greyhound Charter
                          Service on a national basis
                        * In charge of consolidation of Charter Service Sales
                          Offices into four major offices, automating offices
                          into a single on-line computerized system with an
                          open exchange of information through one central
                          computer system in Phoenix, Arizona (completed in 90 days)
                        * Reduced work force over 45% while increasing sales
                          and productivity
                        * Established a Centralized Reservations Center to handle
                          all Tour and Travel features for Company, both
                          domestically and internationally, and reduced workforce
                          by over 40% while increasing sales and productivity
                        * Established training program; developed In-House
                          Training Films
                      Reason for leaving: Transferred to Jacksonville, Florida.

September, 1979   <u>Western Area Marketing Manager</u> - Phoenix, Arizona
     to   Duties and Responsibilities:
February, 1980   * Development of Marketing Plan, advertising and sales
                          in 14 Western States for Company
                        * Development and implementation of schedule changes,
                          service improvement, increasing sales and profits
                        * Reported to Senior Vice President of Marketing
                      Reason for leaving: Accepted position of Vice President,
                                           Charter Service.

May, 1975   <u>Director of Employee Relations</u> - Phoenix, Arizona
     to   Duties and Responsibilities:
September, 1979   * Developed Company's Affirmative Action Program in
                          area of Equal Employment Opportunity
                        * Supervised and assisted Field personnel on National
                          basis with implementation and administration of
                          Company's policies and programs pertaining to EEO
                        * Processed complaints, prepared reports and files for
                          various EEO Agencies
                        * Supervised compliance reviews
                        * Acted as Company representative in preparing and
                          participaing in litigation in connection with Civil
                          Rights cases
                      Reason for leaving: Assumed Western Area Marketing Manager
                                           position.

FREDERICK E. BOWMAN   Page 3

EXPERIENCE
CONTINUED:

1974-1975   <u>Director of Industrial Relations and Personnel</u> -
                    Cleveland, Ohio
                    Duties and Responsibilities:
                      * Assisted in formation, coordination and administra-
                        tion of all industrial relations and personnel
                      * Coordinated implementation of Company's Equal Employ-
                        ment activities and policed following of corporate
                        policies
                      * Represented Division in meeting with Union representa-
                        tives in grievance hearings at arbitration and contract
                        negotiations
                      * Advised Field personnel on industrial relations matters
                      * Member of Algamated Transit Union/Greyhound Lines
                        Contract Interpretation Committee
                    Note: Greyhound Lines, East was everything East of the
                           Mississippi River.
                    Reason for leaving: Two Divisions merged, and I was
                                         transferred to Phoenix, Arizona.

1971-1974   <u>Director of Industrial Relations</u> - Cleveland, Ohio
                    Duties and Responsibilities:
                      * Held grievance hearings and represented Company at
                        arbitration
                      * Analyzed grievances as to location, type and circum-
                        stances to determine ways to avoid grievances and
                        improve employee relations
                      * Represented Company at EEO Compliance Reviews
                    Reason for leaving: Promoted to Director of Industrial
                                         Relations and Personnel.

1969-1971   <u>Director of Tours</u> - Cleveland, Ohio
                    Duties and Responsiblities:
                      * Responsible for development of a Tour Program consisting
                        of escorted tours and independent tours from all points
                        East of the Mississippi to destinations throughout
                        the country
                      * Planned tours, scheduled tours, supervised operation
                        and made reports, including accounting reports
                      * Prepared travel folders and other point of sales
                        material
                    Reason for leaving: Promoted to Director of Industrial
                                         Relations

1968-1969   <u>Director of Special Markets</u> - Chicago, Illinois
                    Duties and Responsibilities:
                      * Represented Greyhound in selling its services to
                        minorities, senior citizens, youth market and other
                        special market groups

FREDERICK E. BOWMAN   Page 4

EXPERIENCE
CONTINUED:
                        * Represented Greyhound at Conventions and other
                          functions of the special interest groups
                        * Explained service and presented Greyhound as a good
                          company and a good neighbor
                        * Scheduled and made media appearances in major cities
                          throughout the country

1964-1968   City Marketing Manager - Detroit, Michigan
                        Duties and Responsibilities:
                        * Supervised Greyhound's sales and marketing activity
                          in Metropolitan Detroit
                        * Selected and supervised Greyhound's Agencies in
                          Metropolitan Detroit
                        * Trained Travel Bureau personnel and personnel in
                          Telephone Information Center in Detroit Terminal

1962-1964   Baggage and Express Agent - Cleveland, Ohio
                        Duties and Responsibilties:
                        * Served as Counter Agent for Greyhound's Package Express
                        * Loaded and unloaded busses
                        * Checked and released baggage

1961-1962   QUALITY SERVICE, INC. - Detroit, Michigan

                        Office Manager
                        Duties and Responsibilities:
                        * Administrative functions of office
                        * Hiring and firing and assigning personnel their related
                          duties

1958-1961   SELF-EMPLOYED

                        Maintenance Engineer
                        Duties and Responsibilities:
                        * Repairing, rebuilding and decorating buildings, including
                          carpentry, plumbing, electrical work and decorating

ORGANIZATIONS: State of Arizona Tourism Advisory Council; appointed by
                        Governor for three years ending in June, 1983
                        State of Arizona, Department of Transportation Venture
                        Team; appointed by Governor, 1982
                        Member of National Tour Association Motor Coach Council, 1983

REFERENCES: Furnished upon request.